# Own Your M.E.D.I.A

I0041673

Prosper Taruvinga

Copyright © 2025

All Rights Reserved

ISBN: 978-1-7641794-0-9

# Dedication

To my clients—

The visionaries, the risk-takers, the ones who refuse to settle. This book is for you, the business owners, carving out a space where profit meets purpose, where success feels as good as it looks. May you build a business that's not only profitable but truly enjoyable.

And to Angela—

For being there since Day 1, through every late-night brainstorm, every breakthrough, and every battle. Your belief has been my anchor, and your presence is my greatest asset. This journey wouldn't be the same without you.

# Acknowledgment

I extend my deepest gratitude to the incredible team at Livelong Digital—both here in Australia and our dedicated colleagues in South Africa—whose unwavering support and expertise have been instrumental in bringing the "Own Your M.E.D.I.A" concept to life.

A special thank you to my fellow BNI members and the vibrant Zimbabwean community in Australia. Your encouragement and belief in my vision have been a constant source of inspiration.

To every guest who has graced The Online Prosperity Show, your insights and stories have enriched our journey and helped shape a platform that empowers others to take control of their media presence.

Together, you've all played a pivotal role in helping me own my media, and for that, I am profoundly thankful.

# About the Author

Prosper Taruvinga is a Zimbabwean-born entrepreneur, author, and digital marketing strategist based in Melbourne, Australia.

As the founder of Livelong Digital, Prosper has dedicated his career to helping service-based businesses—particularly coaches and consultants—generate consistent, high-quality leads and achieve sustainable growth. Prosper's journey from humble beginnings in Chivhu, Zimbabwe, to becoming a sought-after marketing expert is a testament to his resilience and commitment to personal development.

After relocating to Australia, he immersed himself in the world of digital marketing, eventually creating the "Online Prosperity Blueprint," a four-step system designed to help businesses thrive online.

In addition to his work with Livelong Digital, Prosper hosts "The Online Prosperity Show," where he interviews professionals across various industries to share insights and strategies for business success.

His passion for empowering others extends beyond business; he's also known for his engaging speaking engagements and commitment to community development. Prosper lives in Melbourne with his wife, Angela, and their daughters, Kaliyah and Alania.

When he's not working with clients or hosting his show, he enjoys reading, personal development, and exploring new ways to inspire others to "own their M.E.D.I.A" and achieve their full potential. For more information about Prosper and his work, visit livelongdigital.com.au.

# Preface

When I came to Australia 12 years ago, I had nothing but a backpack full of hopes and dreams. I entered this new land as a stranger, and my first job was washing dishes at a restaurant on Lygon Street here in Melbourne. I tried so hard and worked diligently to blend in with everyone. However, soon, I realized that the restaurant needed a social media presence. Without one, it was hard to connect and learn more about the people I was working with. As human beings, we are social creatures. Our little communities and clans keep us safe, protecting us from the invisible saber-toothed tigers that might have us for lunch. There is strength in numbers. We are all wired for social interaction. Melbourne, at that time, was the most multicultural and livable city in the world, yet I felt disengaged and isolated.

Fueled with determination to bridge this gap, I took the initiative and created a Facebook page for the restaurant without my boss's permission. Little did I know that this small act of rebellion would chart the course of my life forever. However, this was not the same sentiment for my boss. He was furious and insisted that I take the page down, saying it would only draw negative reviews. Back then, the internet was an unknown and hardly trusted thing. Never mind the best reasons I would give about the potential of social media. I was fired on the spot for insubordination. I was broken. My hopes and dreams were deleted along with that Facebook page. It hurt so badly. I felt rejected and hopeless. There I was, thinking I was helping. My confidence literally crashed as I tried anything. Then, I quickly found, however, that nothing can stand in the way of an idea whose time has come.

A funny thing began to happen as I waited through the month-long deactivation period of the Facebook page. Influencers began tagging themselves in photos while dining at the restaurant, and the page started to take off. My boss saw the potential. He called me up and asked if I could come back to work, this time handling the social media side of things. I had unwittingly made my first client and used this case study to secure more work with other restaurants and venue centers in the future. This was just the start of my journey.

After three years of apprenticeship, I started my agency, Livelong Digital. The rest is history. I learned that no matter what obstacle gets in our way, it is only temporary. We need to work from where we are to the future we dream of. Waiting until we "have" the life we want before doing what we love is a mistake. We need to take action and grow where we are planted. Nine years later, I work with some of the biggest and most well-known names in Australia. I've received awards for the skills I have in networking, enabling my clients to build lucrative and enjoyable businesses. In 2020, while everyone was coughing into their elbows, I was awarded Networker of the Year by a local Networking Chapter. My family is happier than ever, and I'm living proof that anything is possible if we're willing to work hard and never give up on our dreams. I have also been on National TV and even cried on stage. This was a great experience and an opportunity to thank the teacher who had changed my life. So, no matter what you are going through, this too shall pass. Start now. And never stop trying. I just wanted to connect with people; little did I know I was connecting with my purpose. This was me only 12 years ago. I never thought small, so it didn't matter where I started. Your turn.

Can you remember what you were doing on Boxing Day 2020? I can certainly remember what I was up to. I was working desperately hard to bring up a human at Facebook Support. I first noticed it on Boxing Day: a charge of over $7,000 on our company credit card for Facebook ads. This couldn't be the case because we weren't running any ads. Long story short, they hacked Facebook. The hacker took control of my personal Facebook account, locked us out of the Livelong Digital ads account, and started running ads on our client's accounts in the business suite. I write purposely that Facebook was hacked, not me, because I had two-factor authentication turned on, and I was never asked for the second factor. We called the support Facebook human from Singapore, who turned off our ads account (although it took a complaint to our credit card issuer to get our money back). Simultaneously, Facebook turned off our business page while they "investigated."

Here we are, four years and multiple futile conversations with their support, and they are still "investigating" themselves. The slowly accumulated following on Facebook? Gone. Utterly beyond our reach. Advertising on Facebook? Not a chance. That was how I began my business; from Facebook came my career. All gone. In all five years, I built a business, created for and related to our audience, yet didn't create a single bit of our content outside of the platform. We had been sucked in by the algorithm, and when we lost access, so did everything we had created. The Facebook group with 17k followers and the daily Facebook live videos that were 30 minutes long are all gone. All the five years I had "built a business," poof. Gone. I haven't bothered to go back on Facebook because it doesn't match our plan anymore.

The moral of this story is an old one: It's a high-risk proposition to build your house on someone else's land. That's why everything we do through social media has turned into a secondary factor compared to what we do using podcasts, emails, and our media platform. I have since been able to create assets that I no longer have to worry about, as they are our own. Most people are surprised when they hear it's possible to build your business without relying on social media. Wait a minute, other ways? Yeah. So, if you ever think or feel like you have to use social media to build a profitable and enjoyable business. Let me hit you with some news: I didn't use much social media for my business from years 4-7. Yet, within those same years, my business grew by 25%-50% each year. Maybe we would have grown even more with social media, but the trade-off just wasn't worth it for me. I can't emphasize enough how tired the thought of continuously "posting and being visible" made me feel. Not to mention, it felt like the opposite of the freedom, flexibility, and fulfillment I started my Freedom Business to create.

Another reason out of many that I got into SEO is because if you want to create and give value, but you don't like this whole social media song and dance, there is no better way to do that. Not only that, but people find you because they are interested in what you are offering, not because you were thrust upon them as they aimlessly burned time scrolling through their feeds. So what does that mean exactly? Since they are finding you through the search results, they're much likelier to trust you and your knowledge base. Not to mention the fact that, in a nutshell, SEO is, by and large, one of the most scalable and profitable traffic methods known to man, and while we're partial to SEO, there are many ways you can scale your business without social media around here.

Seven things I've learned since being off Facebook and Instagram: I don't like Instagram that much. I used to. In 2021 and 2022, I posted A LOT. I did a lot of Reels, my face on camera, and the silly lip-syncing. I did it all. I enjoyed it at the time. But now it just feels... stale. Going off Instagram was a conscious decision, not a fear-based decision. Meaning I didn't get off Instagram because I was afraid of being visible or because I was scared of what people thought of me.

I got off Instagram because that fear was no longer in me. I don't need to be on Instagram. Most of my clients come from referrals and SEO. I spent hours optimizing my website and writing blog posts. Better marketing tools in service of those goals are SEO and email marketing.

There might be better marketing channels to serve your business goals, too. Instagram is not a MUST for a business. Social media coaches love to tell you that you NEED to be on Instagram. You don't. It isn't for everyone. And that's OK! Be able to pick your marketing based on how you feel. I don't like what Meta's doing as a company. It feels like you're a slave to Zuck and the algorithm, which doesn't feel good. Now that we have all learned how terrible social media is for us, it becomes pretty challenging to get behind a platform that, without qualms about the content, only encourages its usage. You do not need masses of followers to receive clients. What you need are qualified leads. Qualified leads are those who fit your ideal client profile AND who are looking for your services and can pay you. That means qualified leads are genuinely interested in doing business with you. Social media is not always the best way to increase qualified leads. You're in control here. Businesses existed before Facebook and Instagram. Coaching existed. Even online companies existed! So, it's important to remember that your business can exist without it as long as you set it up so that it can. Remember: You can choose how, what, where, and when you market your business. You're the CEO. If you're feeling beholden to social media, maybe it's time to take a break or at least integrate another marketing strategy into your business. It's your business, and it's your choice. It's time to

**#Own Your Media**

Page Left Blank Intentionally

# Contents

# Chapter 1: The Social Media Trap

## The Illusion of Control

When I first started my business, Livelong Digital, social media felt like a golden ticket. Platforms like Facebook, Instagram, and Twitter were powerful tools, offering direct engagement with my audience and unprecedented reach. It felt like I was in control. I showed up every day for my Facebook Live sessions at 2 p.m. AEST, interacting with my followers in real time. The excitement was intense seeing the engagement, answering questions, and building a community; it was all coming together perfectly. I could practically feel the momentum building as my business grew.

But that sense of control was an illusion. One afternoon, I was preparing for my daily live session when I suddenly found myself locked out of my Facebook account. Panic set in. All the content I had created, all the connections I had made, seemed to disappear in an instant. It wasn't just an account lockout; it was a wake-up call. My business, which had been thriving on Facebook, was suddenly at the mercy of the platform.

I spent weeks trying to get clarity from Facebook's support team, but by the time I regained access to my account, they still wanted me to prove it was me. Now, had Facebook forgotten who the victim was here? Was I not the one whose whole life and business had been taken away? I decided not to bother with the authentication, and the account term of 30 days elapsed. The damage had already been done. The momentum I had built was gone. I had lost credibility, energy, and, most importantly, trust in the platform. At that moment, I realized that while I had been building my business, I hadn't been building a foundation I could truly control. Facebook had the power to determine whether or not my content reached my audience, and in a single moment, that control was ripped away from me.

The truth I learned the hard way is that the power we think we have on social media is largely an illusion. Yes, we can post, engage, and build audiences, but at any given moment, those platforms can change the rules, lock us out, or even disappear entirely. That's when I realized I needed to build something I could truly control. I needed to own my media.

Signs You Might Be Too Reliant on Social Media

Let me ask you this: Do any of these scenarios sound familiar?

- You feel anxious every time Facebook or Instagram changes its algorithm.

- Most of your leads and sales come from social media platforms.

- You find yourself spending more time creating social media content than focusing on your core business strategy.

- A significant portion of your revenue is tied to your presence on social media platforms.

If you've nodded along to any of these points, chances are, you're too reliant on social media. It's easy to fall into the trap, especially when platforms like Facebook, Instagram, and TikTok offer such incredible reach. But when your business thrives on the whims of an algorithm you can't control, you're setting yourself up for a risky future.

Social media promises a world of instant connection, but that promise often comes with hidden costs. You're at the mercy of an ever-changing algorithm, and your content is often buried under a pile of newer posts. You might create valuable content that goes unnoticed simply because the algorithm favors other types of posts. This feeling of being constantly overshadowed can cause unnecessary stress and uncertainty.

Think about it: if your business is built on a platform that can change its rules at any moment, how much control do you really have? The answer is simple: not much. If your audience and revenue are dependent on social media platforms, you're essentially renting space. And when you rent, you have to follow the landlord's rules. But if your business is built on platforms you own, your website, email list, or podcast, those are yours. You control the message, the content, and the audience. Think of it this way: If Elon Musk simply wanted to Tweet, would he have paid $48 million for the platform, or would he have simply downloaded it for free like the rest of us?

## The Algorithm Rollercoaster

Social media algorithms are unpredictable. Take Facebook, for example. The platform's News Feed algorithm has been notorious for its ever-changing nature. In recent years, Facebook made a significant change, prioritizing posts from friends and family over content from brands. While this change improved the user experience, it severely limited the organic reach for business pages like mine. Content that once thrived on Facebook suddenly seemed invisible.

Consider the countless small businesses that built their entire marketing strategy on Facebook. When Facebook decided to tweak its algorithm, these businesses saw their reach plummet.

Their organic engagement, which they had worked so hard to cultivate, vanished almost overnight. Some had to invest heavily in paid advertising just to stay visible. You now have to pay to play. This is the rollercoaster effect of social media. You can be on top one day, riding the wave of engagement, and the next day, you're plummeting into obscurity because the algorithm has changed. When this happens, you find yourself scrambling to catch up, spending more money on ads, creating more content, and working harder than ever, all just to maintain your visibility. Well, I think I do not have the height to go on this algorithm rollercoaster.

The unpredictability of these algorithms means that success on social media is not sustainable in the long term. One day, your content may get tons of likes, shares, and comments, and the next day, it's buried beneath a sea of newer content. For service providers and small business owners, this creates a volatile situation. It's a cycle of feast and famine, never knowing when the algorithm might shift, and your content will be pushed to the bottom of the feed.

## The FOMO Factor

Fear of Missing Out, or FOMO, is one of the most powerful drivers in the world of social media marketing. We see others post, share, and gain followers, and we feel the pressure to do the same. With the constant bell of notifications and the endless stream of content, it's easy to feel like if you're not constantly posting, engaging, and staying visible, you're falling behind.

But here's the reality: FOMO is an illusion. Yes, social media can be a great tool for connecting with your audience, but it shouldn't be the center of your marketing strategy. Social media platforms are designed to keep you hooked, pulling you in with distractions and content overload. But this comes at a cost: your time, energy, and focus.

As business owners, we tend to feel like we need to be everywhere, doing everything at once. We try to keep up with trends, post multiple times a day, and engage with every comment. It's exhausting. But instead of constantly reacting to the pressure of social media, you need to start creating content that resonates with your audience in a meaningful way. Take control of your message and deliver it on your own terms.

What many business owners fail to realize is that there are other ways to build relationships with their audience without being tethered to social media. Instead of chasing likes, comments, and shares, you can create meaningful content that connects with your audience through owned platforms, like your website, email list, and podcast.

## The Psychological Toll

Beyond the technical challenges of relying on social media, there's a psychological toll that's often overlooked. Social media has a way of making us hyper-aware of how others perceive us. Every post, comment, and like is scrutinized, leading to an unhealthy fixation on validation and approval. This constant need for external validation can be emotionally exhausting.

I know from personal experience how draining it can be. Every time I posted on Facebook, I found myself checking for likes, comments, and shares, wondering if people liked what I had to say. The pressure to maintain a perfect image, to always be "on," took a toll on my mental health. This was the hidden cost of my reliance on social media. It wasn't just the time spent creating content; it was the emotional energy I poured into the process, leaving me feeling burned out and depleted.

The signs of social media burnout are clear:

- You feel anxious about posting content.

- You spend excessive time planning and creating social media content.

- You constantly check for likes, comments, and shares.

- You feel emotionally drained after using social media.

If any of this sounds familiar, it's time to take a step back and reevaluate your relationship with social media. It's OK to set boundaries and take control of your time and energy. Social media is a tool, not the foundation of your business.

The Way Forward: Owning Your Media

So, what's the solution? How do you break free from the social media trap and take control of your business? The answer is simple: **Own Your M.E.D.I.A**.

Owning your media means you are in control of your message, your audience, and your content. Instead of relying on platforms that can change their algorithms or shut you out, you create your own channels where you have full control. This gives you the stability and peace of mind that comes with knowing your business isn't at the mercy of someone else's platform. Once you own your M.E.D.I.A, you can plug your content into any platform, such that you USE social media, not social media, *using you.*

In the next chapters of this book, I'll walk you through the steps to take control of your business's future by building your own media platforms. Here's a quick preview of the path forward:

M - Message/ Market

E- Engagement- Education –

D- Distribution- How you reach people and get your products into their hands

I- Ip, Inventory, Ideas

A - Automate- Amplify -Authority

This is how you do it.

1. **Build Your Website**: Your website is your online home. It's a piece of real estate that you own, and it's where your audience can come to find out more about you, your services, and your message.

2. **Start an Email List**: An email list is one of the most powerful tools you can have in your marketing arsenal. It allows you to build a direct connection with your audience without relying on third-party platforms.

3. **Create a Blog**: Share your knowledge and expertise with your audience through a blog. Not only does this help position you as an authority in your field, but it also helps improve your SEO and organic reach.

4. **Start a Podcast or webinar**: These formats allow you to connect with your audience on a deeper level and establish a stronger relationship.

5. **Repurpose Your Content**: Once you have valuable content, don't just let it sit there. Repurpose it across different platforms to reach a broader audience.

By building your own media, you can create a business that's independent, stable, and less vulnerable to the whims of social media platforms. You'll have a direct line to your audience, and you won't be at the mercy of algorithm changes or security breaches.

The Marketing Channel Matrix

To help you visualize your media strategy, I've created a **Marketing Channel Matrix** to show the difference between owned, rented, and borrowed platforms:

| Channel | Owned | Rented | Borrowed |
|---|---|---|---|
| Website | Yes | No | No |
| Email List | Yes | No | No |
| Blog | Yes | No | No |
| Social Media | No | Yes | No |
| Guest Blogging | No | No | Yes |
| Webinars | Yes | No | No |

As you can see, owned platforms like your website and email list are essential for building a business that's sustainable and resilient. Rented platforms (like social media) can help amplify your reach, but they should never be the foundation of your strategy.

It's time to shift the paradigm. Social media is not the enemy; it's a tool. But it shouldn't be the cornerstone of your business. By owning your media, you take back control of your business and your message. This chapter is just the beginning of that journey. In the coming pages, we'll explore practical strategies to help you build and grow your business without relying on the unpredictable whims of social media platforms. It's time to build a business that you own, one where you control your destiny and your growth.

If you ever get stuck throughout the book, come back and scan this QR code and leave me a voicemail.

# Chapter 2: The Real Cost of Being "Connected"

Everyone says, *"You need to be on social media to grow your business."* But no one tells you what that really costs.

It's the advice repeated like a mantra by marketing gurus, business coaches, and even well-meaning friends. Open an Instagram page, post regularly on Facebook, engage with followers on Twitter, and don't forget to make TikToks if you really want to "win" in today's market. It sounds simple, almost effortless—just show up and start building an audience.

But here's what they don't tell you: *social media is borrowed land.*

Imagine spending years building your dream home, only to discover you don't actually own the land beneath it. At any moment, the landlord can change the rules, charge you extra fees, limit your access, or even evict you with no warning. That's the reality of building a business on platforms like Facebook, Instagram, TikTok, and Twitter.

At first, it feels like you're in control. The platform provides access to millions of potential customers, offers engagement tools, and even gives your business a sense of legitimacy. But behind the scenes, you're playing by someone else's rules—rules that can change at any moment, with no regard for how it affects you. These platforms weren't built for small business owners. They were built to serve their own interests, which means their *true* priority is ad revenue, engagement retention, and data collection—not your business growth.

You don't have to take my word for it. Just look at how these platforms operate. Every few months, there's a new algorithm update that drastically changes how content is seen and engaged with. One day, your posts will be thriving and reaching thousands. The next? They're buried under a flood of competing content with no clear reason why.

If you want to play the game, you have to keep up—constantly adapting, constantly guessing, and constantly working twice as hard to maintain visibility. And even then, success isn't guaranteed.

If your entire business depends on these platforms, you don't really own your audience. Facebook does. Twitter does. Instagram does. If one of these platforms disappears tomorrow or you decide you no longer belong there, what will happen to your business?

The answer is unsettling: It disappears along with it.

We've seen it happen before—overnight suspensions, hacked accounts, algorithm updates that make businesses unrecognizable. And still, millions of entrepreneurs continue to build their brands on these platforms, hoping they'll be the exception.

But hope isn't a strategy. *Ownership is.*

This chapter isn't about telling you to abandon social media—it's about understanding its limitations. You should absolutely use social media for reach and amplification. But relying on it entirely is like playing a game of chance where the odds are never truly in your favor.

To see why, let's start with the biggest player in the game—Facebook.

## Facebook (Now Meta): A Shifting Giant with Unpredictable Tides

If there's any platform that demonstrates the illusion of control, it's Facebook.

For years, Facebook has positioned itself as the ultimate marketing tool for businesses. It promised organic reach, real-time engagement, and targeted advertising that could put your brand in front of exactly the right audience. Business owners bought into the dream, investing time, money, and energy into building their presence.

But the dream changed.

In 2021, Facebook rebranded to *Meta*, a move that signaled more than just a name change. It was a shift in focus—a clear message that Facebook was no longer just a social networking platform. It was now a massive, ever-evolving tech conglomerate prioritizing virtual reality, artificial intelligence, and, most importantly, *its own shareholders*.

For business owners, this meant one thing: Facebook was no longer built for them—it was built for Meta's bottom line.

This shift was already evident in how Facebook began treating business pages. Organic reach, which once allowed businesses to engage freely with followers, had been declining for years. Meta's new direction only accelerated this. Now, businesses had to pay just to be seen.

Once upon a time, you could post on Facebook, and your audience would see it. Simple. However, as the platform grew, so did its focus on keeping users *on* Facebook rather than engaging with external businesses.

Enter the algorithm.

The Facebook algorithm determines which posts appear on users' feeds, and its priorities are constantly shifting. Sometimes, it favors video content. Other times, it boosts engagement-heavy posts. And occasionally, it promotes trending topics over personalized content.

For business owners, this means *no strategy is ever stable.* You can spend months perfecting your content approach, only for the next algorithm update to make it irrelevant. This forces businesses into an exhausting cycle of constant adaptation—trying to chase an ever-moving target with no guarantee of success.

The worst part? The algorithm *isn't neutral.* It actively suppresses content that drives users *away* from Facebook. External links, promotional posts, and even certain words (like "sale" or "discount") can get throttled in visibility.

What Does This Mean For Businesses?

- Your posts don't get seen unless they align with Facebook's ever-changing criteria.

- Your reach is artificially limited unless you pay for ads.

- Your engagement depends more on algorithmic trends than on real customer interest.

And even if you play by the rules, there's no guarantee of long-term stability.

Facebook's transformation into Meta wasn't just a strategic shift—it also led to a flood of content creators, businesses, and pseudo-experts competing for attention.

The barrier to entry for business marketing on Facebook is virtually nonexistent. Anyone can start a page, launch a campaign, and call themselves an entrepreneur. This has created an oversaturated environment where credible businesses are constantly battling against low-quality content, spam, and misinformation.

If you've ever felt like your content is getting lost in the noise, it's not just your imagination—it's by design. Facebook's algorithm is built to *prioritize engagement over quality*, which means viral posts, controversy, and sensationalism often get more visibility than genuine, well-researched business content.

For a business owner trying to build trust and authority, this is a nightmare. Your expertise takes a backseat to clickbait and engagement-hacking tactics that have nothing to do with real value.

Beyond the algorithm's unpredictability, there's another major concern—Facebook's enforcement of community guidelines.

While every platform has rules, Facebook's policies have been criticized for being vague, inconsistently applied, and, at times, outright arbitrary.

Accounts have been suspended without clear explanations. Business pages have been demonetized for minor infractions. And during global events like the COVID-19 pandemic, businesses saw their content flagged or suppressed without warning.

When a platform's policies are unclear, it creates a climate of uncertainty. Business owners hesitate to post certain content out of fear that it might get flagged, leading to self-censorship that stifles growth.

The final nail in the coffin? Once you've built your business on Facebook, leaving isn't easy.

Unlike a website or email list, where you own your audience and data, Facebook locks everything within its ecosystem. If you ever decide to transition to another platform, you can't take your followers with you.

Your customer base? Stuck.

Your content? Gone.

Your reach? Reset to zero.

For those who have spent years investing in Facebook as their primary marketing channel, this realization comes too late. They wake up one day to find that they're no longer in control of their audience, their visibility, or their revenue.

And the truth is, they never really were.

**So, what's the alternative?**

We'll explore that in the next sections, but first, let's look at another major platform that has become both an opportunity and a trap for business owners—Instagram.

# Instagram: Beauty Over Substance and the Cost of Keeping Up

If Facebook is the loud, ever-changing giant, Instagram is its younger, flashier sibling — all about looks, trends, and appearances. On the surface, Instagram feels like the perfect platform for businesses: visual, dynamic, and engaging. But scratch beneath that glossy filter, and you'll find a platform that demands constant performance, endless reinvention, and an exhausting chase for validation. When I first started using Instagram for my business, I thought it would be a fun way to showcase behind-the-scenes moments, client wins, and snippets of wisdom. But before long, I realized I had entered a never-ending race where the finish line kept moving.

Instagram has been overrun by influencers, and I don't say that with judgment; I just observe. Anyone with a smartphone and a bit of confidence can position themselves as an authority, whether they have the experience or not. And with every new influencer popping up, the feed becomes more crowded, the bar for content quality rises, and small businesses like mine get lost in the shuffle. You're not just competing with your industry peers; you're competing with fashion models, fitness coaches, travel bloggers, and viral meme accounts. The algorithm doesn't care who provides value — it cares who can stop a user's thumb from scrolling.

# An Algorithm That Changes Like the Weather

One month, it's all about carousel posts. The next, it's Reels. Then Stories. Then collaborations. It feels like trying to hit a moving target in the dark while balancing on a tightrope.

I can't count how many hours I've spent learning new formats, testing hashtags, analyzing engagement rates, and trying to understand why a post that should've resonated fell flat. Every time you think you've figured out the game, Instagram changes the rules.

And here's the kicker: even when you do everything "right," you're still at the mercy of an algorithm that's designed to prioritize content that keeps users *on Instagram*, not content that benefits your business.

## Monetization Roadblocks

Instagram makes it incredibly hard to convert attention into action. You get *one* clickable link in your bio. That's it. No clickable links in captions. No easy way to direct people to multiple resources. So you find yourself juggling "link in bio" tools, constantly updating links, and hoping your audience actually clicks. And if you want more reach? You guessed it — *pay to play*. Organic visibility has taken such a hit that even your most loyal followers rarely see your content unless you're boosting posts or running paid campaigns.

Instagram demands perfection. It's not enough to post a quick photo and a caption. You need professional-level images, expertly crafted copy, perfectly timed hashtags, and consistent engagement. That means replying to comments, responding to DMs, and showing up on Stories — every single day.

And if you miss a few days? Out of sight, out of mind. The platform quickly forgets you, and regaining traction is an uphill battle.

There's also the temptation — and risk — of shortcutting through purchased followers or engagement pods. But these "hacks" only hurt in the long run. The algorithm quickly catches on, and your reach plummets even further. Plus, fake followers don't buy your products or invest in your services. They're just empty numbers that inflate your ego and deflate your results.

Instagram looks glamorous from the outside. But for business owners, it's a treadmill — the faster you run, the more you stay in the same place.

### Twitter/X: Loud, Fast, and Shallow

If Instagram is all about visuals, Twitter (now X) is about speed. Quick thoughts, hot takes, and viral threads dominate the platform. However, for business owners, it can feel like trying to deliver a keynote speech in the middle of a shouting match.

Twitter wasn't built for businesses; it was designed for journalists to share news in real time. Somewhere along the way, brands jumped in, trying to use the platform to engage customers. And while some have succeeded, most of us quickly learned that 280 characters are rarely enough to convey meaningful messages.

I tried using Twitter to connect with my audience, share insights, and join conversations. But I constantly felt like I was either shouting into the void or scrambling to keep up with trends that had a lifespan of minutes.

## The Noise Problem on Steroids

Twitter is the definition of crowded. Millions of tweets are sent every hour. Breaking news, memes, celebrity drama, political debates — all fighting for attention. Even if your message is valuable, it's fighting for oxygen in a room full of smoke machines and air horns.

The platform thrives on immediacy. If you're not tweeting multiple times a day, you're forgotten. But if you tweet too much, you're noisy. Finding the balance is exhausting.

## Freedom of Speech Without Freedom of Reach

Twitter champions free speech, but that doesn't mean everyone sees what you say. Shadow-banning — the quiet suppression of certain accounts or topics — is real. You might be posting valuable content, but if it doesn't fit into the platform's current "acceptable" narrative, it quietly disappears from people's feeds.

I remember crafting thoughtful, well-researched threads that went completely unnoticed while others posting controversial or clickbait content went viral. It's disheartening, and it forces businesses to choose between staying true to their message or playing the game.

## Fake Engagement and Bot Armies

Twitter has become a playground for bots and automation tools that can inflate engagement numbers artificially. But once again, these shortcuts don't lead to real business growth. The platform is flooded with accounts that exist solely to retweet and inflate numbers without offering any real value.

## The Rebrand to X: A Change Without Clarity

When Twitter became X, it wasn't just a cosmetic change. It symbolized a shift in vision — one that left business owners guessing. The platform's purpose became murky. Was it still a microblogging site? A news aggregator? A town square? Nobody really knew. And for businesses trying to build consistency, uncertainty is the enemy. You need a stable, predictable environment to communicate with your audience and drive action. Twitter/X is anything but stable.

In the end, using Twitter for business felt like standing in the middle of a highway, holding up a sign, hoping someone slows down long enough to read it — and knowing they probably won't.

## The Financial Pitfall: My $250K Lesson

There's theory, and then there's reality. I learned this the hard way when my entire business presence — years of effort, content, and connections — vanished in the blink of an eye.

You hear stories of people losing access to their accounts, but you never think it'll happen to you. I didn't either. But when it did, it wasn't just inconvenient — it was catastrophic.

In a single moment, my Facebook account, the very platform where I had built momentum, trust, and a steady stream of income, was locked down. And not just locked — frozen, inaccessible, and held hostage by vague policies and a faceless support system that couldn't care less about the livelihoods they disrupted.

I tried everything: appeals, identity verification, contacting support, and even looping in friends of friends who worked in tech. But the clock kept ticking on Facebook's 30-day deactivation window. Every passing day felt like watching sand slip through my fingers.

When that window closed, so did the door on a substantial portion of my business. I didn't just lose followers or "engagement metrics." I lost clients. I lost scheduled speaking opportunities. I lost collaborations. And most painfully, I lost revenue.

By the time the dust settled, I estimated the financial blow to be around $250,000. And trust me, that number doesn't just hit your bank account — it hits your confidence, your sense of security, and your ability to lead.

But here's the kicker: *The platform didn't care.*

There was no phone call, no personalized email, and no avenue for real conversation. Just automated responses, hoops to jump through, and silence. For a business owner who had poured so much into building a genuine community, it was a brutal wake-up call.

I had been playing a game where the house always wins.

And the worst part? I had allowed it. I had built my business on someone else's rules, someone else's turf. I didn't own my audience — Facebook did. And when they took it away, I realized I had no backup plan.

This wasn't just a financial lesson; it was a philosophical one. If your entire income relies on platforms you don't control, you're not building a business — you're gambling. The stakes are high, and the odds are not in your favor. And while money can be replaced, time and trust cannot. Rebuilding after that kind of loss is exhausting, demoralizing, and slow. Some people never recover. I was determined to be one of the few who did. But that journey started with one painful but liberating realization: *I would never again build my house on borrowed ground.*

## Why This Matters: Borrowed Ground and Unwritten Rules

At this point, you might be thinking,

> *"Well, that's your story, but I'm careful. I'm diversified. I'm playing smart."*

I thought the same thing.

But here's the truth no one tells you: Social media platforms are not your partners. They're your landlords. And just like any landlord, they can change the locks, raise the rent, or sell the property — all without your input.

Every single post you make, every follower you gain, every DM conversation you have — it all exists in a rented space. You do not own it. You are allowed to use it under conditions that can change at any time for reasons you may never fully understand.

And these platforms? They're not static. They evolve constantly — sometimes without logic, sometimes without fairness, and always in their own best interest.

It's not just about algorithms; it's about power dynamics. You're essentially a pawn on a chessboard where billion-dollar companies move the pieces however they like. They're playing for ad dollars, shareholder satisfaction, and political positioning. You're just trying to connect with your audience and grow your business — but in their world, you're not the priority.

Let me put it this way: If they can shut down a global platform like TikTok for 24 hours in a major country, imagine how quickly your business page can be silenced without notice or explanation.

I've seen colleagues lose their entire audience overnight due to sudden bans. I've watched brands that spent years cultivating communities disappear because they posted something the algorithm didn't "like."

The ethical implications are troubling. The financial risks are real. But what cuts deepest is the realization that you never had control in the first place.

You've been told, *"Go where the people are."* But what happens when those platforms decide they don't want *you* there anymore?

This isn't about doom and gloom. It's about awareness. Because once you see the game for what it is, you can finally stop being a player in someone else's system and start building your own.

I want you to imagine this:

Instead of constantly worrying about algorithm changes, shadow bans, or platform shutdowns, what if you had an audience you owned? An email list that couldn't be taken away from you. A website where you set the rules. A podcast where you control the message, the schedule, and the content.

The platforms aren't going anywhere. And yes, they can be powerful tools for amplification. But they should never be your foundation.

Relying on rented platforms is like building a castle in the sand. It looks impressive until the tide comes in — and trust me, it *always* comes in.

I'm not telling you this to scare you. I'm telling you this because I've lived it. I've lost what I thought was unshakeable. And I've rebuilt — stronger, wiser, and on solid ground.

The question is: Are you going to keep gambling with your business, or are you ready to own your empire?

When you're ready, I'll show you how to start.

## The Wake-Up Call: How I Became a Swiftie

After losing everything I had built on Facebook, I found myself sitting in my office in complete silence. I stared at my computer screen, overwhelmed by a sinking sense of loss — not just financial, but emotional. My business, my momentum, my credibility — all of it felt like it had vanished into thin air.

I sat there, wondering where even to begin. How do you start from scratch after losing what took years to build? How do you rebuild trust, confidence, and presence in a digital world where platforms hold all the power?

That's when I stumbled across an article that changed everything for me.

It was about Taylor Swift.

She had famously lost control of her master recordings — her life's work — to a record label that made decisions without her consent. But instead of fighting for something that was no longer hers, she made a bold decision: she re-recorded her entire music catalog. Track by track, album by album, she rebuilt her legacy on her terms.

She didn't beg for permission. She didn't wallow in defeat. She took action. She took ownership.

Reading that story hit me in a way I didn't expect. If someone like Taylor Swift, with all her fame, resources, and influence, could lose control of her own creations — and yet choose to rebuild stronger — then what excuse did I have?

She didn't just accept the loss. She turned it into an opportunity.

That moment was my turning point. I realized I had been doing business backward. I had spent years creating, building, and nurturing — but all on platforms I didn't own. Platforms that could shut me out without warning. Platforms that I had no control over.

Taylor Swift's story wasn't just about music. It was about ownership. It was about reclaiming control. It was about taking back what was rightfully hers and ensuring that no one could ever take it from her again.

And in that moment, I knew I had to do the same.

I couldn't keep building on someone else's terms. I couldn't continue placing my business in the hands of platforms whose goals didn't align with mine.

I had to own my media.

That single realization reshaped my entire approach to business. It lit a fire inside me, a determination not just to rebuild but to build smarter, stronger, and on the ground I could actually call my own.

The journey wasn't going to be easy, but it was clear. I needed to stop being a tenant and start being a landlord. I needed to stop chasing algorithms and start creating content that lived on platforms I controlled. I needed to build something that couldn't be taken away from me — ever again.

Here's the thing: this isn't just *my* story. It's the story of thousands — maybe millions — of business owners who are building their dreams on foundations they do not own.

We've been conditioned to believe that social media platforms are the magic bullet. That if we just post enough, engage enough, and play by the rules, success will follow. But those rules are written in pencil — and the platforms hold the eraser.

They can change community guidelines overnight. They can throttle your reach, shadow-ban your content, and limit your visibility, all without warning or explanation. One day, your posts are reaching thousands; the next, they're seen by a handful. And you're left scrambling, wondering what you did wrong.

The truth? You didn't do anything wrong. You just forgot who owns the game board.

These platforms are not designed for your business stability — they're designed for their own survival. They care about their shareholders, their engagement metrics, and their ad revenue. Your business is collateral damage in their pursuit of bigger profits and more control.

And the most dangerous part? Most business owners don't even realize they're playing a losing game.

They invest time, money, and energy into building massive followings on Instagram, Facebook, TikTok, and Twitter. But those followers aren't *theirs*. They belong to the platform. You can't export them. You can't move them. And when the platform changes its rules — or shuts down — your audience disappears with it.

That's why relying on these platforms as your primary business vehicle is like building a castle on sand. It might look impressive for a while, but eventually, the tide comes in.

We've already seen it happen:

- TikTok is facing bans in major markets.

- Facebook shutting down business accounts without warning.

- YouTube channels are being demonetized overnight.

- Instagram influencers lost visibility because the algorithm "decided" they were no longer relevant.

And each time, those business owners are left scrambling, wondering how they'll recover.

But here's the most important truth I want you to take away from this: *you don't have to play by those rules anymore.*

The moment you realize that social media platforms are just tools — not foundations — is the moment you start building something that lasts.

I'm not saying don't use social media. I still do. But I use it on *my* terms. I use it as an amplifier for content that lives on platforms I own.

My website? That's mine.

My email list? Mine.

My blog? Mine.

My podcast? Mine.

And guess what? When you own the platform, you write the rules.

This is not just a business decision. It's a mindset shift. It's about moving from being a renter to being an owner, from being a pawn in someone else's game to building your own chessboard.

I've lived the pain of losing everything overnight. I don't want that for you.

So, if you're reading this and relying solely on rented platforms, consider this your wake-up call.

Because the platforms will change, the algorithms will shift. The rules will be rewritten.

The question is: will you still have a business when they do?

If you're ready to stop gambling and start building something solid — something no one can take from you — then keep reading.

The next step is learning how to own your media, build your ecosystem, and take back control.

And trust me, once you do, you'll wonder why you ever built on borrowed ground in the first place.

## The Fragility of Digital Empires: What Took Years Can Vanish Overnight

I know what it feels like to pour years into building something only to watch it disappear in an instant. But here's the part that really stings — you realize it was never really yours to begin with.

We've become so accustomed to measuring success by follower counts, likes, and viral moments that we forget how fragile those metrics really are. These platforms — Facebook, Instagram, Twitter, TikTok, YouTube — are not digital kingdoms where you reign supreme. They are empires built by someone else, and you are merely a subject within their walls.

And subjects don't get to make the rules.

Think about how often you hear stories of accounts being hacked, suspended, or outright banned. Influencers who built their entire careers on one platform suddenly disappear, left with nothing but a sobering "violation of community guidelines" notice. Businesses that rely on predictable traffic from Facebook or Instagram find themselves invisible after a quiet algorithm update.

It's not rare. It's not random. It's built into the very DNA of these platforms.

And here's the truth: what took you years to build — all the trust, all the relationships, all the hard work — can be wiped out in minutes.

A platform tweak.

A security breach.

A policy change.

A server outage.

A political decision.

You name it — any of these events can hit you out of nowhere.

We saw it happen with the TikTok bans. One day, creators with millions of followers were thriving. The next, they were in limbo, wondering if they'd have a platform the next morning.

And if you think these disruptions only happen to small players, think again. Massive brands have faced shadow bans. Major influencers have had accounts shut down. Even prominent news organizations have been throttled by algorithms designed to prioritize *engagement* over *accuracy*. The platforms don't care how big you are. They care about how much control they can exert.

If they can do it to the giants, they can do it to you.

That's why building your business *on* these platforms is like building a sandcastle during high tide. You can sculpt, design, and admire your creation all you want, but the waves are always coming. And when they hit, they don't ask permission.

Here's the hardest part to swallow: no one will warn you.

There are no red flags, no countdown clocks, no friendly heads-up. It just happens. One day, everything is fine. The next, you're locked out, throttled, buried.

And the real question becomes: if your digital empire falls, can you rebuild it?

For those who've built wisely — with owned media at the core — the answer is yes.

For those who haven't, the fall can be permanent.

## Pawns in a Bigger Game

I want to paint a picture for you.

Imagine a giant chessboard. The kings and queens are the big tech companies: Facebook (Meta), Google, YouTube, Twitter/X, and TikTok. They control the board. They decide the moves.

And you? You're a pawn.

Now, that might sound harsh. But think about it.

You spend hours, days, and even years crafting content, building engagement, and following their rules. You think you're part of something grand — building a business, a brand, a movement. But at the end of the day, you are expendable.

Platforms don't make decisions with you in mind. They make decisions for shareholder returns, market dominance, and regulatory strategy.

If you're suddenly caught in a policy change or a political controversy, your presence on the board is insignificant. The game goes on — without you.

Look at what happened during the 24-hour TikTok ban. Millions of creators who had made the platform their home were suddenly pushed off the board. Their videos, their followers, their revenue — frozen. All because someone higher up decided it was the right move.

And it's not just TikTok.

Facebook's algorithm changes have buried thousands of businesses that once thrived.

YouTube has demonetized creators who built careers on the platform.

Twitter has become an unpredictable arena where even verified accounts can lose reach overnight.

The worst part? There's no recourse.

You can't call someone and plead your case. You can't negotiate your way back onto the board.

You're either playing by their rules — or you're gone.

But here's the good news: pawns have one advantage.

They can cross the board and become a queen.

You're not stuck being a pawn forever. The moment you decide to build your own platform, your own media, your own ecosystem — you take yourself off *their* board and start building your own.

That's when you become the king or queen of your business. That's when you set the rules, define the strategy, and control the moves.

I learned this the hard way. But once I stopped playing on someone else's chessboard and built my own, everything changed.

The stress of algorithm changes? Gone.

The fear of shadow bans? Gone.

The uncertainty of policy updates? Gone.

Because on my board, I decide what content gets seen. On my board, I decide how and when to engage with my audience. On my board, I build assets that no one can take from me. I'm not telling you to quit social media. I'm telling you to stop letting it own you. Use it. Leverage it. But never build your entire business on it.

The platforms will continue playing their game. The question is: will you remain a pawn, or will you start building your own board?

## From Tenant to Owner

After everything I had gone through — losing my content, losing revenue, and watching years of effort evaporate — I finally understood something I had ignored for too long. I wasn't a business owner in the digital world. I was a tenant. And tenants live at the mercy of their landlords. I had been paying rent to Facebook in the form of my time, effort, and ad dollars. I had been dancing to Instagram's tune, constantly creating content that served *their* engagement goals rather than my business objectives. I had been trying to make my voice heard in Twitter's crowded, noisy arena. All of it was built on land I didn't own.

The funny thing is, I had always told myself I was in control. I had convinced myself that building an audience on social media was just a good business strategy. But the truth? I had been building someone else's asset. I was investing my best ideas, my most valuable content, and my energy into platforms that profited from my work — and gave me nothing guaranteed in return.

When that realization finally hit me, it stung. But it also empowered me. I thought about Rockefeller. I recently watched a documentary about how he built his empire — not by relying on others but by owning the means of production, distribution, and delivery. He didn't rent. He didn't borrow. He built. He owned. He controlled every piece of the pipeline. And suddenly, it all clicked. I needed to become my own Rockefeller. I needed to stop dancing to the rhythm of these platforms and start building something *I* controlled from end to end.

It was no longer about creating content that fit into someone else's box. It was about building my own box — shaping it the way I wanted, filling it with content that mattered, and inviting my audience into a space that I owned. That meant building my website, building my email list, starting my podcast, hosting my webinars on platforms I controlled, and creating an ecosystem that couldn't be wiped out by someone else's algorithm. The platforms could still exist. I could still use them. But they would no longer *own* me. They would become tools — not foundations. And that shift in thinking changed everything.

The story of losing $250,000 wasn't just about financial loss. It was a turning point that forced me to confront a truth most business owners eventually learn the hard way: if you don't own it, you can't protect it. I had spent years building on borrowed ground, following someone else's rules, hoping they would be kind to me. But hope is not a strategy. It took losing everything to realize that real security — real business freedom — comes from ownership. It comes from building assets that no one can take away. It comes from having direct access to your audience without a gatekeeper. It comes from creating systems that work for *you*, not the other way around.

Taylor Swift re-recorded her catalog and took back ownership of her music. Rockefeller built pipelines so that he didn't have to rely on anyone else's infrastructure. And now, it was my turn. The question I ask you is: are you ready for it to be *your* turn, too? Because here's the truth: if you're building on social media alone, you're playing a game where the rules will always change — and rarely in your favor. If you're building on platforms, you don't control. You're one policy update away from losing everything.

But if you start now — building your own media, owning your platforms, nurturing your audience on *your* terms — you'll never have to play that game again. You won't panic when algorithms change. You won't scramble when bans happen. You won't lose sleep wondering if your business will still exist tomorrow. You'll have solid ground beneath your feet. You'll own your media. You'll own your message. You'll own your audience. You'll own your future.

In the next chapter, I'll share exactly how I began this process. I'll take you behind the scenes to explain what it means to own y*our M.E.D.I.A.* and how you can start building a business that no platform can ever take away from you because the world doesn't need more tenants. It needs more owners. And that owner can be you.

# Chapter 3: Own The Means Of Production

At some point, I realized I was doing business like a tenant in someone else's building — paying my dues, following the rules, hoping not to get evicted. It worked for a while, but deep down, I knew I wasn't in control. Then, I came across the story of John D. Rockefeller — a man who didn't just sell oil. He owned the entire pipeline.

Rockefeller didn't depend on someone else to refine or transport his product across the country. He built the refineries, the railways, and the distribution channels. He created a system where every single part of the process — from extraction to delivery — flowed through his own hands. That's when it hit me: *he didn't just sell a product. He owned the means to deliver it.*

And that right there? That's what shifted my thinking. I realized our digital media ecosystem is the modern-day equivalent of Rockefeller's pipelines. In today's world, information is the oil. Content is the currency. And whoever controls the flow — controls the value.

Until then, I had been producing great content, but it flowed through pipelines I didn't own. I was showing up on platforms that weren't built for me, weren't designed to protect my business, and certainly weren't interested in giving me long-term stability. These platforms were built to keep me dependent, and I didn't see it for a while. But once I connected the dots — once I saw how owning the *infrastructure* was just as important as owning the *product* — I couldn't unsee it.

Rockefeller didn't make his wealth from selling barrels of oil. He made it by controlling how that oil moved — who had access to it, where it went, and what happened to it once it left the ground. And that's exactly what we need to do in business today.

We need to control how our message moves.

We need to determine who sees it, how often they engage with it, and what journey they take after that first interaction.
We need to stop letting platforms set the pace and start building our own distribution systems — our own pipelines.

This chapter is about stepping into that ownership mindset. Not just owning your product or service but owning the *process* of how it reaches your people.

So before we get into the nitty-gritty of how to build your media, I want you to keep one picture in mind: Rockefeller, standing at the edge of a rail line he owned, watching barrels of oil from his own fields get loaded onto trains he controlled, headed to factories he had built.

That's not just business. That's legacy.

And it starts when you stop renting visibility and build your own.

## The Birth of an Idea: My Turning Point Toward Media Ownership

The idea didn't arrive as a sudden flash of brilliance. It wasn't something I found in a mastermind session or a weekend retreat. No, the idea that would change everything — the seed that would grow into this entire philosophy of owning your media — came from a moment of frustration, a quiet hour in my office after a chaotic loss, and an unexpected story about a pop star.

I was sitting in that heavy silence that followed a personal earthquake. My Facebook account was still locked. My audience was unreachable. My content — years of effort — is gone. I was supposed to go live that day, like I always did at 2 p.m., to speak to a growing community of entrepreneurs, coaches, and small business owners who had come to rely on my voice and guidance. But this time, the platform didn't let me in.

I wasn't even angry anymore. I was just tired. The kind of tiredness that sits in your bones.

To distract myself from the heaviness, I opened my laptop and started scrolling — not through social media this time, but through blogs. That's when I found it. A

45

headline that stopped me: *"Taylor Swift to Re-Record Her Entire Catalog."* I clicked out of curiosity more than anything. What I read sparked something deep inside me.

Taylor Swift, one of our time's most successful recording artists, had lost control of her master recordings. Years of work, all the hits, all the albums — technically belonged to someone else. And instead of fighting to get them back, she decided to do something revolutionary: start again. Recreate every song, one by one. Take full ownership of her sound, her legacy, and her brand.

It wasn't just a PR move. It wasn't a stunt. It was a declaration: *I will never let anyone else control my message again.*

That hit me hard. Here was someone at the top of her game, with all the influence and reach in the world, still vulnerable to someone else's control. And what did she do? She didn't complain. She didn't launch a smear campaign. She quietly and strategically took ownership.

That's when the gears started turning.

I thought back to all my hours crafting content for Facebook, Instagram, and Twitter. All the videos, captions, lives, and threads. How much of that did I actually own? How much of it could I control? The answer was sobering: *none of it.*

It made me look at my business through an entirely different lens. What had I really been building? A community — yes. A brand — maybe. But it was all sitting on land I didn't own, propped up by infrastructure that could vanish at any time.

That Taylor Swift article gave me permission to question everything.

Then I remembered something else I had watched a few weeks earlier: a documentary on Rockefeller. That story, too, had stirred something in me, but I hadn't connected the dots until now. Rockefeller didn't just sell oil. He built the pipelines. He owned the refineries. He made sure no one could block him, delay him, or take from him what was his.

Suddenly, it all aligned. If I wanted to build something that would last — something that no hack, no ban, no algorithm could shake — I had to build the *pipeline*.

Not the oil. Not the container. The pipeline.

Owning your media is building your own pipeline.

From that day, I stopped seeing social media as my business hub. I started seeing it as a billboard — useful for attention but not a place to live. You don't move your whole family into a billboard. You build a home somewhere stable.

*My website? That's my home.*

*My email list? That's my phonebook.*

*My blog and podcast? Those are the dinner tables where I sit and connect deeply with the people who care.*

The moment I made that shift in my thinking, everything began to change.

Suddenly, the frantic need to beat the algorithm vanished. The stress of having to be everywhere at once — gone. The burnout from trying to keep up with content trends, growth hacks, and viral formulas dissolved.

Instead, I began to think like an owner. I started creating with purpose, not pressure. I started building systems around what *I* valued, not what the platforms told me to value.

I began mapping out what it would look like to create my own media ecosystem that served *me* and *my audience* directly. I listed the channels I truly owned:

- My website.

- My email subscribers.

- My personal network.

- My own videos are hosted on my terms.

I realized that the most sustainable businesses — the ones I admired — didn't chase social media. They used it to drive people back to their own space. They created a magnetic field that pulled people in, not a funnel that pressured them.

And so I committed:

I would stop building castles in the sand.

I would stop renting Visibility.

I would start constructing an empire that no one could delete, censor, or "lock me out" of.

That decision became the foundation for everything that followed.

Now, here's the thing — I'm not Taylor Swift. I don't have a global fanbase or a label dispute worth millions. But I do have something just as important: *a message that matters to the people I serve.*

And if that message gets silenced because I didn't take ownership of its delivery — I've failed.

I realized that owning your media isn't about ego. It's about stewardship. It's about protecting the message you've been entrusted with.

The same way Taylor protected her songs.

The same way Rockefeller protected his oil.

The same way I had to protect my voice — and you must protect yours.

I had no idea this realization would grow into a philosophy, a framework, a movement. But it started with one blog post, one documentary, and one hard-earned lesson.

So when people ask me, *"Why do you care so much about media ownership?"* this is what I tell them:

Because I've been locked out of my own business before.

Because I know what it feels like to have no power over what you created.

Because I refuse to build anything that can be taken from me again.

This isn't just about content. It's about control.

It's about leverage.

It's about leadership.

And it starts with a mindset shift — the same shift that came to me one quiet afternoon when I finally saw what needed to change.

That was the birth of the idea.

The spark.

The line in the sand.

From here on out, everything would be built differently.

## What It Means to Own Your Media

In today's fast-paced digital world, one of the most overlooked assets in any business is control — not just over the product or service you offer, but how that offering is communicated, delivered, and sustained. That's where the idea of "owning your media" truly begins to matter. It's more than just a buzzword or a clever strategy — it's a fundamental shift in how entrepreneurs should be thinking about visibility, engagement, and longevity in the marketplace.

Most people don't realize their digital presence is fragile until something goes wrong. And when it does, it hits hard. A shadowban here, an algorithm update there, and suddenly, your reach plummets, your community becomes silent, and your content disappears into the void. You might still be publishing, but nobody's hearing you. You're speaking, but the room is empty. That's the reality of building your business on someone else's land — you're visible only when it serves the platform's agenda, not yours.

Owning your media is the antidote to that fragility. It's about reclaiming control over your voice, your message, and your ability to connect with your audience without a third party standing in the way. When you own your media, you're no longer at the mercy of external platforms deciding who sees what, when, and why. Instead, you're creating a structure — an ecosystem — that you can rely on, refine, and expand as your business grows. At its core, owning your media means having your own infrastructure in place. That starts with your website — your digital home base. Unlike a social feed that refreshes every few seconds and buries your best content beneath endless scrolling, your website is where your brand lives in full color. It's a place where your message is uninterrupted, your story unfolds on your terms, and your value is positioned with intention. Visitors aren't distracted by ads, trending memes, or viral videos. They're there for you — and only you.

Then there's your email list, which is often the most underappreciated yet powerful tool in your arsenal. Think of it as your direct line to the people who have already said, "Yes, I want to hear from you." These aren't passive followers hoping to stumble upon your content — they're subscribers who've chosen to stay connected. And that matters. Because when the rules change, as they always do, your email list stays with you. It's portable, personal, and protected from the whims of any algorithm.

Add to that your blog, podcast, and YouTube channel — these are your owned platforms where your ideas can breathe and evolve. They're not driven by trends or designed to manipulate short-term attention. Instead, they're rooted in value. They build trust over time. They position you as a consistent presence in the lives of those who are looking for guidance, insight, or transformation. What owning your media does, in essence, is shift your business from reactive to proactive. You're no longer reacting to every update, every trend, every new platform feature. You're building something sustainable. Something strategic. Something that doesn't collapse the moment your reach dips or your account gets flagged. Because let's face it — reach is fleeting. Trends pass. However, relationships built on trust through owned and consistent channels will carry your business through seasons of change.

And no, owning your media doesn't mean abandoning social media altogether. We'll talk more about that soon. The point isn't to disappear from platforms where your audience already hangs out. The point is to stop depending on them. Stop treating them like your primary residence when they're really just the billboards that lead people home.

The difference is subtle, but it's everything. When you post on Instagram now, it's not out of desperation to be seen — it's a strategic move to direct people back to your podcast episode, webinar, blog, or opt-in page. When you share a video on YouTube, you're not hoping to win the algorithm lottery. You're offering value that lives elsewhere, too — on your site, in your funnel, and inside your community. You're using these tools with purpose, not depending on them for survival.

What makes this approach so powerful is that it gives you permission to build your business *your way*. Without external pressure to fit into formats that don't suit your voice. Without compromising your brand just to chase clicks. Without getting caught in a loop of short-form content that burns you out and never moves the needle.

Because when you own your media, you're not just creating — you're curating an experience. You're not just broadcasting — you're building a connection. You're not just collecting followers — you're nurturing a community.

That community knows where to find you — not just on a platform that might disappear tomorrow, but in a space you've built for them. A space where they're heard, valued, and engaged beyond the superficial. That's where loyalty comes from. That's where impact begins to take root.

It's important to understand that building this kind of ecosystem takes intention. It won't offer the instant gratification that social media often dangles in front of us. But what it does offer is resilience. And in today's world, that's worth more than likes, shares, or retweets ever could be.

So if you've been feeling stretched thin by the never-ending content treadmill... if you've been wondering why you're not seeing the traction your work deserves... or if you're simply ready to build something that's built to last — owning your media is the next move. It's not about doing more; it's about doing what matters, where it counts, and for the people who need it most.

Because, in the end, your ideas deserve a platform that's as solid as the vision behind them. Your message deserves a home that the next policy update won't tear down. And your business deserves to grow on the ground you own, not one rented month-to-month from tech giants who don't even know your name.

That's what it means to own your media.

And once you make that shift, there's no going back.

Absolutely — here's the full, detailed write-up for:

## The Cost of Poor Messaging: The Dentist Who Lost the Sale

Years ago, when I first moved to Australia, I found myself in a situation that taught me more about marketing and messaging than any business book ever could. At the time, I was just settling into my new life, figuring things out one day at a time.

Like many people trying to adjust to a new environment, I began noticing things about myself that I hadn't given much attention to before — including the gap between my front teeth. Now, to give you some context, this gap is something quite common where I come from. In many African cultures, it's even considered a mark of beauty or character. But living in a new place, surrounded by different beauty standards and professional settings, I started feeling self-conscious about it. Not because someone said something but because I was trying to fit into a world that seemed to expect a polished, uniform smile — the kind you see on dental posters or in Zoom meetings where appearances matter. So, I did what most people would do. I started exploring the possibility of fixing it.

I walked past a local dental clinic every day on my way to work. It was a tidy, modern-looking practice, clearly well-kept. Outside, in big, bold letters, was a sign that read: **"New Patients Welcome."** Simple. Professional. Direct. But something about it made me keep walking.

Not once did I walk through those doors. Not even to inquire. Not even to ask about options. And here's the kicker — I had a genuine need. I was *ready to buy*. I even looked into treatment options online. I was willing to make the investment — and believe me, the quote I eventually got elsewhere came to a whopping $14,000 AUD. That's no small amount. It was a serious decision. Yet this practice I walked past daily never earned my business.

*Why?*

*Because their message didn't speak to me.*

Let me explain.

That sign — *"New Patients Welcome"* — was technically accurate. It was polite. It was professional. But it didn't make me feel like *I* was the person they were talking to. I didn't identify as a "patient." I wasn't sick. I wasn't in pain. I wasn't looking for a checkup or a root canal. I was just a guy looking to feel more confident about his smile. That gap in my teeth wasn't a medical issue but a self-esteem one. I wasn't seeking treatment — I was seeking transformation.

Therein lies the fatal flaw of poor messaging: when businesses speak from their perspective instead of the customers', they become invisible.

You see, what the dentist saw was a clinical service. What I was looking for was an emotional outcome. They focused on what they do — *dentistry* — rather than what

I wanted — *confidence*. They used their industry's language, not their audience's.

And this happens far more often than most entrepreneurs realize.

We fall in love with our product. We obsess over our process. We talk in terms of features, qualifications, certifications, and technical terminology. But none of that matters if your audience doesn't see themselves in what you're saying. If your message doesn't touch their desires, frustrations, or aspirations — they'll keep walking, just like I did. And you may never even know how close you came to landing the sale. So, let's look at the hidden cost here. That dental clinic didn't just lose me. They lost the $14,000 I represented — and potentially the dozens of others just like me who walked past their office without ever stepping in. All because their message wasn't aligned with the market they were trying to serve.

Imagine if the sign outside had said something like:

**"Want a Smile That Feels Like You Again?"**

**"Ready to Look More Confident in Every Zoom Meeting?"**

**"Transform Your Smile, Not Just Your Teeth."**

Any one of those phrases would have made me pause. Maybe even turn around. At the very least, it would have made me feel like *they understood me* and that they saw what I saw — not just a gap, but a missing piece of confidence. That, my friend, is what marketing should do.

And this isn't just about dentists.

If you're a coach, consultant, creative, or service provider of any kind, ask yourself: Are you using industry language that makes *you* sound credible... or customer language that makes *them* feel seen?

Here's what happens when your message isn't aligned with your market:

- **You attract the wrong people.** People who don't fully value your offer or who are confused about what you do.

- **You miss out on qualified leads.** Prospects who were ready to buy but couldn't tell you were the right fit.

- **You become forgettable.** In a world of endless noise, only messages that *resonate* will be remembered.

- **You devalue your work.** By failing to highlight the transformation, you're competing on price and convenience — not impact.

The worst part? You won't always see the lost opportunities. People who didn't feel spoken to don't leave a comment. They don't reply to your emails. They don't click unsubscribe. They just fade away. Silently. And you're left with a stream of content that sounds good in your head but lands flat in the real world.

This is why aligning your message with your market is one of the most important — and often overlooked — steps in building your media ecosystem.

When you own your media, you're not just reclaiming *where* your content lives. You're refining *how* it speaks. It's not just about independence — it's about *intimacy*. It's about building a brand that doesn't need to shout because it knows exactly what its people need to hear. Your message should answer the questions your audience is already asking — sometimes silently. It should acknowledge their pain, validate their dreams, and offer a way forward. And most importantly, it should do it in their language. Not yours.

So, take a lesson from the $14,000 the dentist never earned. Don't just put a sign out that says "New Customers Welcome." That's not enough anymore. You need to say what your customer is actually feeling. You need to speak to what they're truly hoping for. You need to reflect on the future they want and show them how you'll help them get there.

That's the cost of poor messaging — not just missed sales but also *connection*.

The good news? You can change that starting today.

## Benefits of Owning Your Media: Why This Approach Works

There's a quiet confidence that comes with knowing that your business can keep moving, even when the online landscape shifts. When you've built your message on solid ground — on platforms you own, control, and understand — you stop reacting to every algorithm change or policy update. Instead, you operate with clarity, stability, and purpose. That's the real benefit of owning your media. It's not just about creating content — it's about building something that *lasts*. Let's get practical here. When you own your media, you're creating more than just a marketing strategy — you're building *infrastructure*. You're laying down digital bricks that support not just visibility but *sustainability*. Platforms will come and go, and trends will rise and fall, but your website, email list, and podcast are assets that grow with you. They're not beholden to anyone else's roadmap. They don't disappear in a policy update. And they certainly don't ask you to pay just to talk to the people who've already said they want to hear from you.

One of the most immediate benefits of owning your media is **security**. You're no longer vulnerable to being locked out of your community. You don't have to wake up in fear that your Instagram account has been hacked, your Facebook page has been suspended, or your YouTube videos have been demonetized for some vague violation you didn't even understand. When your business lives on your own site, your followers are subscribers on your email list, and your videos are embedded on your landing pages, you have *resilience*. You have protection. You have peace of mind.

But security is just the beginning. Ownership brings **stability**.

You can plan. Strategize. Build long-term campaigns without worrying that the platform's priorities will shift next quarter and render your entire approach obsolete. You can launch a podcast series knowing the format is yours to shape. You can publish a blog post that continues to bring in organic traffic for years — not hours. This is content that compounds. It works while you sleep. And the best part? The rules don't change on you every time the platform updates its software.

There's also a psychological benefit — one most entrepreneurs don't even realize until they've made the switch. When you move from platform-dependent to platform-independent, you feel something else: **freedom**. Creative freedom. Time freedom. Mental freedom.

You no longer feel the pressure to constantly perform, post, and engage just to stay relevant. You're not stuck in the loop of creating content that disappears the next day. Instead, you're building a library. A living, breathing archive of your ideas, your expertise, and your value — all in one place, under your control. And that does something powerful to your energy. It shifts you from burnout to alignment. From hustle to flow.

Then there's **scalability** — another massive advantage of media ownership. When your content is systematized, searchable, and organized within a framework you've built, you can repurpose it with ease. You can automate onboarding sequences through your email list. You can create evergreen funnels that run without needing your constant attention. You can publish one piece of content and break it down into ten others — all pointing back to your ecosystem. Instead of reinventing the wheel every week, you're reinforcing a wheel that turns without friction.

And perhaps most importantly, owning your media builds **authority**.

Think about the brands you trust most. The voices you return to. The leaders who've left a lasting impression on you. Chances are, they're not just putting out bite-sized content that disappears in 24 hours. They've built depth. They've earned your attention through consistent presence on platforms that reflect their values. When you consistently show up in your own space with your own message, your audience begins to see you differently. Not just as another expert in the feed but as a *leader*. Someone with a mission. A point of view. A brand worth following — and buying from.

Now, let's be clear. This isn't about ego. This isn't about trying to prove how important you are. It's about **positioning**. Positioning matters.

Because when your brand lives only on borrowed platforms, you're always part of the crowd. You're one post away from irrelevance. But when you start owning your message and curating the experience your audience has with you — everything changes. You go from interchangeable to *indispensable*. From background noise to *trusted voice*. And that's where influence is born.

Here's another key point: owning your media improves your **customer experience**. When your audience interacts with you through a journey you've designed — not one dictated by platform mechanics — they feel more connected. They feel seen. They feel like part of something. You're no longer throwing content into the wind, hoping it lands. You're creating intentional pathways that guide your audience from interest to trust to conversion — naturally, respectfully, and effectively.

And in a world overloaded with content, *experience* is what makes the difference.

Let's also not forget the **financial** implications. When you own your media, you reduce dependency on paid ads and boost the lifetime value of every lead. You build assets that can be monetized in multiple ways: courses, memberships, books, speaking engagements, affiliate opportunities, and more. Your website isn't just a digital brochure — it becomes a business engine. Your email list isn't just a collection of contacts — it's a revenue pipeline. This is how you move from hustle to *harvest*. When people say, "The money's on the list," they're not wrong. But that list needs to live somewhere you control. Otherwise, your income is as unstable as your follower count. Finally, owning your media is a **legacy move**. It's how you create something bigger than your next post. It's how you leave a digital footprint that lasts beyond a campaign or a quarter. It's how you write your story on your terms — and leave a trail that others can follow, learn from, and be inspired by.

Because that's what this is all about, isn't it? Not just getting noticed but *making a difference*. Not just showing up but *standing out*. Not just building an audience but *leading a movement*.

When you own your media, you claim that power. You stop waiting for permission. You stop chasing attention. You stop playing small.

You start building something that belongs to you.

And that's where the real magic happens.

## Plug and Amplify: Social Media as a Distribution Tool, Not a Home

Now that we've walked through why owning your media gives you clarity, stability, and long-term success, it's time to make something clear: social media still matters — but it's not your home. It's your megaphone.

Let me explain.

Social platforms are brilliant for reach. They're the street corners of the internet — loud, busy, full of potential customers walking by. If you shout the right message at the right time, people might stop. They might even listen. But you're still on rented land, no matter how many likes or follows you gather. You don't own the pavement you're standing on. The rules can change tomorrow. The algorithms can shift. The audience can vanish.

So the solution isn't to abandon social media — it's to *reposition* it in your business model. When you shift your mindset and treat social media as a distribution channel, not your business headquarters, everything becomes more intentional. You stop creating content for the sake of visibility and start crafting content that invites people back to your world — the one you control.

Think of it like this: your media platforms (your website, blog, podcast, or email list) are your *home base*. That's where your best content lives, your brand voice is clearest, and your customer journey begins and ends on your terms. Social media is the road sign pointing to that home. Its job isn't to hold your entire business — it's to *bring people to it.*

Let's use an example. Say you publish a blog post on your site. It's thoughtful, well-written, and packed with insights your audience needs. You then share a snippet of that post on LinkedIn or Instagram — just enough to spark curiosity. Maybe you could even record a short video sharing one powerful takeaway from the article. You include a link. You direct people back to your blog. What you've just done is amplify your owned media through rented channels. You've used social media to create a doorway — not a destination.

This shift is powerful because it changes the kind of content you create. When you're not trying to "beat the algorithm," you stop obsessing over trends and gimmicks. You stop measuring success by likes and start focusing on depth. You create with more meaning. More intention. More impact.

And here's another benefit: when your primary content lives on platforms you own, you can guide the *entire* experience. You can introduce lead magnets, segment email lists, offer personalized resources, and build automation that nurtures people over time. Social media can't do that. It wasn't built for it. It's built to keep people *there* — scrolling, watching, and endlessly distracted.

And that's another important point: social platforms don't want people leaving. That's why posts with external links get throttled. That's why engagement drops when you try to redirect traffic off the platform. But when you own your media, you're no longer fighting to hold attention in someone else's living room. You're inviting people into *your* space — where the conversation gets deeper, the experience becomes richer, and the trust begins to compound.

Still, let's not downplay social media's advantages. It's where attention already exists. Billions of people are there. It's noisy, yes — but the crowd is real. So, treat it like a microphone rather than turning your back on it. Let it echo your message, but never let it contain your mission. Use it strategically.

- Use **Instagram** to share visual stories and lead people to your email list.

- Use **Facebook groups** to spark community and then guide people to your deeper offers.

- Use **Twitter/X** to test ideas and link back to full insights on your blog.

- Use **TikTok** to deliver bite-sized value and direct viewers to a podcast where you go deeper.

Each platform becomes a channel — but the real destination is always your *owned* media.

This also takes the pressure off. You no longer feel the constant need to post five times a day to stay relevant. Instead, you create cornerstone content — timeless, valuable pieces that live on your site or newsletter — and use social media to breathe new life into it again and again. You repurpose intentionally, not reactively. A single podcast episode can become an Instagram carousel, a YouTube short, a LinkedIn article, and an email story. The ecosystem feeds itself.

And here's the kicker: you become algorithm-proof when you do this well. If Facebook goes down for a day, you're not scrambling. If TikTok gets banned or Instagram changes its format, you're not starting over. Why? Because you never gave them the keys to your business in the first place. You built something resilient and used platforms *by design*, not by default.

The ultimate goal is this: social media should serve your mission, not shape it. It should be the lighthouse that draws people to your shore — not the boat that leaves you drifting out at sea.

And this shift isn't just technical. It's philosophical. When you move from chasing trends to creating from your core message, you start attracting the right people. You build community, not just followers. You build loyalty, not just likes. You build *equity*, not just exposure.

Let me leave you with this: if you use social media to amplify what you've built, not to define who you are, you'll always be in control.

So use the billboard. Speak on the street corners. But when people look you up — make sure there's a home waiting for them.

## M Is for Message and Market: Speaking with Clarity, Relevance, and Resonance

At the heart of every thriving business — whether it's a solo consultant or a multimillion-dollar enterprise — is a simple, timeless truth: **people respond to messages that sound like they were meant for them**. Not for a general crowd. Not for a faceless audience. For *them*.

That's what this first letter of the M.E.D.I.A. framework stands for: Message and Market. If you want to build your own media — media that actually moves people — you need to start here. No content strategy, no clever automation, and no viral hack will work if your message doesn't land where it matters most: the hearts and minds of the people you serve.

Let's start with the **message**.

Your message is not just your tagline or your elevator pitch. It's the thread that runs through everything you do — your website, your videos, your emails, your content, your offers. It's the emotional core of your business. It answers the question, *Why should anyone care?*

And to answer that well, you need to get out of your own head and step into the shoes of your ideal client. What do they care about? What keeps them up at night? What are they dreaming of, struggling with, craving, avoiding, searching for?

Too often, we talk about our product or service as if that's what matters. But people don't buy products — they buy **outcomes**. They buy feelings. They buy the transformation your product represents.

Think back to the dentist's story. I didn't need a "dental plan." I needed *confidence*. The message wasn't off because the service was wrong — it was off because it didn't speak to what I was really looking for. I wasn't identifying as a "patient" looking for medical help. I was someone searching for a better version of myself. And that's how your message should function: it should bridge the gap between your audience's pain and their desired transformation.

The key here is **relevance**. You have to meet your audience at the exact moment they're feeling the friction in their life — not a step before, not a step after. This is why understanding your **market** is equally important.

Your market isn't just a demographic. It's not "women ages 25 to 45" or "business owners making six figures." That's surface-level. A real market is built on psychographics — beliefs, aspirations, struggles, habits, and worldviews. The emotional landscape. The silent stories people tell themselves about who they are and what they need. When you speak to those stories, you don't just get attention — you earn trust.

But to do that, you must listen before you speak. What language does your audience use when they describe their problems? What phrases appear in their Google searches, late-night journal entries, or rants they share with close friends? If you can find that language — and reflect it back — you create immediate resonance.

There's a saying in my native Shona language:

*"Ndikataura neChishona, ungangandinzwe?"*

Roughly translated, it means, "If I speak in my language, will you understand me?"

That one sentence contains the whole game of marketing.

If you speak in industry jargon, clever copy, or "branding language" that feels distant, you'll lose people even if your offer is great, even if you're the best in your field. Because if your message doesn't speak their language, they simply won't hear you.

But they will lean in if you show up and speak clearly — with empathy, insight, and honesty. They'll feel seen. Understood. Safe. And once someone feels understood, they're far more open to being guided.

Here's a practical example. Say you're a health coach. You might think your message is, "I help women improve their gut health through functional nutrition." But your audience isn't walking around saying, "I wish I could improve my gut health." They're saying, "I'm tired of feeling bloated after every meal," or "Why can't I lose weight even though I'm eating clean?" Your job is to translate your expertise into the everyday language of *their experience*.

When you do this well, you create what I call **resonant messaging**. It's not just relevant. Not just informative. Resonant — the kind of message that vibrates in someone's chest and makes them say,

*"This is exactly what I've been looking for."*

And here's something else to keep in mind: clarity always wins over cleverness. Always.

You don't need the perfect slogan. You need a clear promise. A clear transformation. A clear connection. Confusion is the enemy of conversion. If people don't "get" what you do in the first few seconds, they'll scroll away, click off, or close the tab. But if you make it obvious — if you show them the before-and-after picture they're already holding in their head — they'll keep reading. They'll come closer. And that's when trust begins.

Another overlooked element of message and market is **positioning**. You need to know where your offer fits in the minds of your audience. Not every product is urgent — but every product must be *contextual*. Are you the aspirin for a headache, the vitamin for long-term health, or the personal trainer that gets people results when they've already tried everything else? Positioning yourself properly also means justifying your audience's failures — not in a condescending way, but with compassion. You acknowledge that they've tried before. You validate that it hasn't worked — not because they're lazy, but because they didn't have the right method, support, or timing. And now, you're here with a better way.

This is how trust builds before the sale. It's how credibility is earned. You're not just showing up as an expert. You're showing up as a **guide** — someone who knows the terrain, understands the pitfalls, and can lead them to where they want to go.

And let's not forget the emotional component of the market. People aren't just looking for solutions — they're looking for **belonging**, **certainty**, **identity**, and **relief**. They want to feel empowered. They want to feel smarter, stronger, more capable, more free. Your message isn't just words — it's an experience. A mirror. A path forward.

So before you ever create a piece of content, before you ever write an email or script a video, ask yourself:

- Who am I speaking to — *really?*

- What do they want?

- What's in their way?

- How can I say what they're feeling before they even say it themselves?

If you can answer those questions with precision, your message becomes magnetic.

And when your message is magnetic, your market will move toward you — not because you chased them down, but because they *felt* something.

That's the first part of building your media. Nail your message. Know your market. Speak their language, solve their problems, and show up like the answer they've been searching for.

Once you've aligned your message with your market, stepped into your audience's world, and spoken in a way that makes them feel truly seen, the next natural step is creating *momentum*. And that momentum doesn't come from constant output. It comes from **connection**.

Connection is where real influence begins. And in today's world, connection is currency.

But not just any currency — **social currency**. The kind that people trade in conversations, share in group chats, and pass along in DMs. Social currency is that invisible value people feel when engaging with your content — the kind that makes them say, "You need to check this out," or "This reminded me of you." When someone shares what you've created not because you asked them to but because it makes *them* look informed, insightful, or helpful — that's social currency at work. And the best part? You don't need to manufacture it. You just need to make your content meaningful enough that people *want* to share it. That means providing value that transcends utility. It's not just "useful" — it's **relatable, emotionally resonant,** and **conversation-worthy**.

If you want to own your audience, you have first to understand how people share. People don't just share tips — they share identity. They share values. They share things that make them feel smart, funny, or aligned. And that's your opportunity. When your message doesn't just inform but *influences how someone sees themselves*, they become an amplifier for your brand.

Now, let's zoom out for a moment.

Owning your media is not about creating content that just "performs well" — it's about creating content that helps people **belong**. That speaks to something inside them. That gives them language for something they've been trying to express. Because when you help people articulate their struggle — or better yet, their *hope* — they'll bring others to your table. They'll become carriers of your message.

This is where we bring in the idea of **Dunbar's Number**.

Robin Dunbar, a British anthropologist, found that the average person can maintain stable social relationships with about 150 to 250 people. That means every person who connects with your content — every follower, listener, subscriber — has their own web of influence. Their own audience. Their own reach.

So when you write, record, or post, you're not just speaking to one person. You're potentially speaking to their **entire circle** — friends, co-workers, family, even strangers on a group thread. That's the ripple effect of resonance. That's the power of owned media paired with strategic sharing.

And here's the secret: when your media is **structured with community in mind**, it becomes more than just content. It becomes a movement.

But how do you actually create content that fuels this kind of community?

Start by making it **repeatable**. Can someone easily repeat your message in a conversation? Can they explain what you do — not in business terms, but in simple, sticky language? Can they share one of your quotes, hooks, or frameworks and look brilliant doing it? If the answer is yes, you've created social currency.

Then, make it **referable**. Is your site easy to navigate? Can people share your podcast, blog, or lead magnet without confusion? Is your opt-in link clean and memorable? The easier you make it for people to pass your content along, the more likely they are to do it. Finally, make it **relatable**. Strip away the industry jargon. Tell stories. Use metaphors. Be human. People don't share perfection — they share what feels real. When you speak with clarity and authenticity, people see themselves in your words. That's what gets talked about. That's what spreads.

There's something else here, too — and it's often missed.

Creating audience ownership isn't just about content — it's about **care**. Real care. The kind that shows up in your tone, your consistency, your responsiveness. When people feel that you *actually care* about helping them — not just selling to them — they'll stay with you longer. They'll root for you. They'll buy from you not because you pressured them but because they *trust* you.

That trust is what turns cold traffic into a loyal community. That care is what makes a reader become a subscriber, a subscriber becomes a customer, and a customer becomes an advocate.

And when that happens, your business stops relying on marketing hacks and starts thriving on **relationships**.

Let me offer a final perspective.

If you do this well — if you build media that speaks with clarity, provides genuine value, and invites your audience to engage — you'll find something beautiful happens. You'll no longer feel like you're shouting into the void. You won't be chasing metrics just to validate your work. Instead, you'll hear back from people. They'll email you. Message you. Stop you at events. They'll say, *"Your post said exactly what I've been feeling."* Or *"That podcast episode helped me take the next step."*

And that's when you'll know you've shifted from content creator to *trusted voice*. From marketer to *messenger*.

That's the true power of owning your media — not just broadcasting but *belonging*. Not just creating visibility but building a village. One voice, one message, one relationship at a time.

If you ever get stuck throughout the book, come back and scan this QR code and **Join The Media Moguls Club**.

# Chapter 4: Create Your Unique Value Proposition and Positioning

Now that you've pinpointed who your market is — the people you're meant to serve, those whose problems you understand deeply — the next step is to decide what to say when they're finally listening. This is that moment. The one where everything changes, not because something dramatic happens in the world around you, but because something shifts inside you. You no longer show up online just to make noise. You show up to make meaning. You're not here to just sell — you're here to serve, to lead, and to build something that lasts.

This chapter will walk you through what it means to have a **compelling and differentiated value proposition** — a message so clear and so aligned that it becomes the cornerstone of everything you create. We'll also dive into how you position yourself in the marketplace in a way that not only captures attention but builds trust. Because let's face it: attention is cheap, but trust is priceless.

We live in a world where distraction is a currency. Notifications pull us in twenty directions. Social media offers a thousand voices a minute. But amidst all the noise, there is always room for one clear voice — one grounded message that speaks with authority and heart.

That's why this chapter is here to help you develop. And before we get into tactics, let me say this: if you're reading these words, you're already doing what most people never do. You've shown up for your growth. You're not flipping through this like another how-to manual. You're here because you want more depth, direction, and *freedom*. You're ready to build a business that's both profitable and enjoyable. You're ready to show up both online and in your life — fully, fearlessly, and clearly.

You see, many people buy books like this and never open them. Some skim the first chapter and forget about the rest. Others read through and do nothing. But *not you*. You're still here, leaning in. That alone is proof of your readiness.

Your transformation has already begun.

I want you to imagine, for just a moment, the ripple effect of what you're about to build. The content you'll create. The people you'll help. The impact you'll have — not by going viral, but by being *valuable*. Not by being loud but by being *clear*. Not by chasing trends but by crafting a voice so true and consistent that people start asking,

*"Who is this person?"*

And here's what they'll say when they find out:

*"That's someone I can trust."*

But trust starts with clarity.

So here's what we're going to do in this chapter: we're going to help you articulate what makes you different. What makes you right for the people you're meant to serve? We're going to help you stop hiding behind vague slogans and start speaking directly to the hearts and minds of your audience. We're going to make sure that when people finally give you their attention — when they lean in and listen — you'll know exactly what to say.

And it starts with this: your value proposition is not a line of clever copy. It's a statement of purpose. A promise. A declaration that says,

*"I understand your struggle, I've walked the road before you, and I've built something that can help you walk it too."*

You're not just building a business. You're building a movement.

And movements don't start with noise. They start with **clarity**.

## Developing a Compelling and Differentiated Value Proposition

Let's get to the core of it.

If the previous chapter was about finding your people — the market you're meant to serve — then this chapter is about knowing what to say to them when you have their attention. This is the part most businesses rush through. They get excited by the tools, distracted by the trends, and start creating content before they ever get clear on the most important thing: **Why should anyone listen to you?**

That's the question your **value proposition** answers.

Your value proposition isn't your elevator pitch. It's not a cute slogan, and it's not the words on your About page. It's deeper than that. It's the essence of what you bring to the table. The reason someone would say, *"Yes, that's exactly what I've been looking for."* It's the promise that sets you apart from everyone else in your space — not because you're louder, but because you're *more aligned.*

Here's the thing: most people online today are speaking *to* their audience. They're posting content for content's sake. They're saying things like, "Join my program!" or "Work with me!" but they haven't taken the time to figure out why anyone should care. And so, nobody listens. The message floats by like noise in a busy feed.

But when you craft a **compelling and differentiated value proposition**, you're not just adding to the noise — you're offering *clarity.* You're giving your audience a reason to stop scrolling. You're giving them *hope* that someone finally understands their specific struggle.

And the key word there is specific.

Generic messages don't build trust. Generic promises don't convert. If you say, "I help people grow," that's nice — but so does every coach, consultant, and brand trying to make a difference. But if you say, "I help first-time course creators launch their first digital product in 90 days without tech overwhelm or burnout," now you've got my attention.

Because that's **specific**, that's **targeted**. That's **useful**.

So, how do you build a value proposition that hits like that?

Start by asking yourself the hard questions:

- What exactly do I do for my audience?

- What is the tangible outcome they get when they work with me?

- What makes my process, approach, or perspective unique?

- Why am I the *right person* to help them through this?

And here's a simple trick that works every time:

**Speak to the version of you from five years ago.**

Why? Because the person you were then is very likely the person you're trying to help now. You know their fears. You know their excuses. You know, the thoughts that kept them stuck. And more importantly, you know what helped them move forward. That's your gold. That's your story. And when you bring that clarity into your value proposition, people feel it. They trust it. They say, *"This person gets me."*

Let's make this real.

Imagine your audience is arriving at your doorstep. You've invited them into your home — not for a hard pitch, but for a real conversation. What would you tell them? What problem would you promise to solve? What results would you stand behind? And how would you say it in a way that feels warm, confident, and rooted in experience?

That's your value proposition.

Here's a practical framework to help you shape it:

**"I help [specific audience] achieve [specific result] without [specific pain or obstacle]."**

For example:

- "I help new coaches get their first three paying clients without running ads."

- "I help working moms lose weight without giving up their favorite foods."
- "I help service-based business owners reclaim 10+ hours a week using automated systems."

The clarity here isn't just attractive — it's *liberating*. For you and for your audience. Because when you know exactly what you offer and who it's for, every email, post, and piece of content you create becomes easier. More intentional. More effective.

And that's what we're doing here. We're simplifying the complex. We're cutting through the fog. We're making your message *undeniable*.

But before we move on, let's be real: not everyone is going to get it right away. You might have to test your message. Refine it. Tweak the words. That's okay. This isn't about getting it perfect on the first try. This is about getting **closer** with every draft. Every email. Every conversation.

The more you show up and speak with clarity, the more your audience will lean in and say,

*"That's exactly what I needed to hear."*

And isn't that the point?

So, write your value proposition like a whisper to someone who's been waiting to hear it. Not a shout to the world — a whisper that lands like a lifeline.

And from here, we'll begin building everything else on top of that foundation.

## Positioning, Pricing, and Perception: The Story People Believe

Once your value proposition is clear — once you've put words to what you offer and who it's for — the next step is to make sure it actually *lands*. And for that, you need to shape the story around your offer. Because people don't buy based on features or logic alone. They buy based on their story about what your offer means.

That's where **positioning** and **pricing** come in.

Let's begin with positioning.

Positioning is about what your audience *feels* when they see your brand. It's the space you occupy in their mind. Are you an accessible expert? The premium problem-solver? The down-to-earth guide who's been where they are? Or the sharp strategist who gets results fast? The way you position yourself informs everything — from your messaging tone to your pricing structure to the testimonials you highlight.

It's not about pretending. It's about *aligning perception with value.*

You've probably seen two people offer the same type of service — let's say they're both business coaches. One charges $250 for a 6-week program, the other charges $7,000. Same outcome on paper. But the positioning is completely different. One might be focused on accessibility and serving beginners, the other on elite transformation and high-commitment clients. Neither is wrong. What matters is that the **story matches the substance**.

Now, let's talk about pricing — the most misunderstood part of the positioning equation.

Most people price based on what others are charging. Or worse, they price based on what they think their audience can afford. But here's the thing: **your pricing is part of your brand story.** It communicates something, whether you realize it or not.

Low pricing might say, "I'm new," "I'm uncertain," or "I'm trying to get anyone to buy." Premium pricing might say, "I'm worth it," "This is exclusive," or "You're investing in results." And everything in between tells its own story, too.

The question isn't "What's the right price?"

The question is, *"What do I want my audience to believe about the value I provide?"*

And that brings us to perception — because value lives in your customer's mind. It's not about what you *think* you're offering. It's about what they *believe* they're getting. If your pricing, your message, your packaging, your tone — if those things don't align with the story in their head, they'll either walk away or question your legitimacy.

Here's a simple way to test your positioning and pricing alignment:

Imagine your customer has a credit card statement. There's a line for groceries. A line for insurance. A line for Netflix. And then — there's a line for your product or service.

Ask yourself:

- Would they feel proud of that purchase?

- Would they need to justify it to their partner or boss?

- Would they remember what they got out of it?

- Or would it be one of the first expenses they'd cancel the next time they needed to tighten the budget?

Because that's the difference between being a *cost* and being an *investment*.

And to become the latter, you need to weave a story — a story of transformation, of possibility, of real value — around your offer. You need to answer every buyer's unspoken question: *"Is this for someone like me? Is this safe? Is this worth it?"*

Let's get even more grounded with a metaphor.

Think of a Timex and a Rolex. Both tell time. Both can sit on your wrist. But one sells for $50, the other for $5,000. The difference? It's not the function. It's the **story**.

Timex says: "We're reliable. We're simple. We're accessible."
Rolex says: "We're legacy. We're excellent. We're timeless status."

Both serve different markets. Both are positioned *perfectly* — for the audience they're meant to reach.

So, what story is your pricing telling?

Are you giving people clarity and confidence — or are you leaving them confused, wondering if you're really the person to trust with their pain, their dreams, their money?

Positioning is not just about bold colors and branding buzzwords. It's about *emotional congruence*. When your message, tone, pricing, and delivery align, it creates a sense of safety for the buyer. They don't just hear your pitch — they *feel* the resonance.

And this is where authenticity becomes your superpower. The best place to create content and position your offer is *the person you were five years ago*. That version of you knows the struggle. Knows the confusion. Knows what it feels like to doubt everything and yet still want more. Speak to them. Price for them. Position yourself as the solution you wish you'd found.

Because here's the truth: people don't just want to buy something. They want to *believe in something*. They want to believe they're making progress and that they're choosing well. This time, it will be different. And your positioning — done right — gives them that belief.

So, as we move forward in this chapter, I want you to hold this close:

**You're not just selling a service. You're offering a shift. A new chapter. A better story.**

Make sure the way you present your offer honors that truth.

## Providing Value to Three Key Groups

A sustainable business doesn't just serve customers. It creates value across the board — for *yourself, your audience*, and *the broader ecosystem you operate in.* If you want to build a business that endures, a business rooted in generosity and real returns, then you need to make sure you're not just chasing transactions — you're building an engine of value creation.

Let's break that down.

### 1.    Value to Yourself: Profit and Sustainability

Let's get one thing straight: your business exists to make a profit. That's not selfish — that's smart. If your business is not profitable, it cannot sustain itself. And if it cannot sustain itself, it cannot serve. You can't pour from an empty cup — not financially, not creatively, and certainly not emotionally.

So before you guilt yourself into discounting your services or undervaluing your time, ask: *Is this business creating value for me?* Am I paying myself? Am I designing offers that allow me to grow, rest, and reinvest? Am I building something that can withstand seasons of uncertainty — or am I constantly surviving off the next sale?

If your pricing, your process, or your positioning is bleeding you dry — it's time to change that. You need a business that pays you for your brilliance, not one that punishes you for caring.

Profit is not the goal — it's the result of doing the right things for the right reasons.

## 2.    Value to Your Customers: Relevance, Results, and Relief

Next up: your customers. You exist because of them. Not in the abstract, not as "leads" or "traffic" — but as real people with real problems, looking for real transformation. So ask yourself: *Are my products or services solving a real problem? Are they making life better, easier, or more joyful for the people I serve?*

This is where the value proposition from earlier starts to take root. Your job isn't to overwhelm your audience with everything you know. It's to offer clarity. It's to say,

*"I've got you. I've been where you are. And I've created something that will help you get where you're trying to go."*

That's not just value — that's *relevance*. Relevance is everything in a noisy world.

When people feel seen and supported by your work and experience the benefit of your message, they don't just become clients. They become fans. They tell others. They stick around. And that is how you build something bigger than just a business — you build a brand people trust.

### 3.    Value to Everyone Else: The Ripple Effect of Real Business

And finally, the third group: *everyone else your business touches.*

This includes your team (even if that's just your future team), partners, collaborators, and even your community. When you run a business with integrity — when your messaging is honest, your pricing is fair, and your service is excellent — you create **ripples**.

Think of the podcast you record that helps someone land their first client.

Think of the blog post that inspires someone to leave a toxic job.

Think of the testimonial that shows someone it's possible to heal, grow, or start over.

These things might not show up on your profit and loss sheet, but they matter. They are the unseen dividends of a business built on purpose.

And when your business creates value for others — it creates **goodwill**. It earns you word-of-mouth referrals, long-term collaborations, and opportunities that no algorithm can take away. You stop chasing visibility and start attracting *trust*.

Your work should pay you well. It should solve problems for your people.

And it should leave a wake of good wherever it goes.

If you're missing even one of those elements, something's off. You're either underpricing yourself, missing the mark with your audience, or not connecting your business to a broader sense of purpose. Fixing that isn't just a branding decision — it's a **foundational reset**.

This chapter is not about temporary engagement hacks. It's about establishing a lasting position in your market — by showing up with value in every direction. Because when you do, your audience starts to say what every great brand wants to hear:

*"They're the real deal. They've helped me. I trust them."*

And when someone trusts you, they'll follow you — not just once, but for years.

## The Five Whys Exercise: Uncovering Your Business Core

In business, clarity isn't a luxury — it's a necessity. And as you grow your audience, sharpen your offer, and begin crafting messages that carry weight, one essential truth rises to the surface: *If you don't know why you're doing what you're doing, no one else will either.* That's where the Five Whys exercise comes in — a deceptively simple, profoundly powerful tool that helps you strip away the noise and reconnect with the soul of your work.

Here's the idea: you begin with a basic statement about what your business does. Then, like a curious child, you ask "why" — not once, but five times. And each time, you go a layer deeper. You challenge yourself to look beyond the surface-level answer and explore what truly matters to your customers and *you*. This exercise helps uncover the emotional heartbeat behind your business — the part that gets you out of bed when the numbers aren't growing or when the algorithm decides to go rogue. Let's say, for example, you run a hair salon. On paper, that's straightforward. You style hair. But when you apply the Five Whys, you'll discover something richer hiding just beneath the surface. You might start by saying, "I provide hairstyling services." That's the first layer. Ask yourself why that matters. "Because people feel good about themselves when they look their best." A little deeper. Why does *that* matter?

"Because when people feel confident, they show up better in their lives and relationships." And why is that important? "Because self-confidence gives people the courage to pursue opportunities they might otherwise shy away from." Keep digging. "Because too many people are living small lives, held back by insecurity when they're capable of so much more." And finally: "Because everyone deserves to feel powerful and proud in their own skin."

Now, you're no longer just a hairstylist. You're a **confidence architect**. A guide helping people reconnect with their best selves. That is the true core of your business — and it changes everything. It changes how you write your website copy, how you interact with clients, how you price your services, and how you position your offer. Suddenly, it's not about the haircut. It's about the transformation. The identity shift. The internal freedom that comes from external change. And this isn't just for service-based businesses or feel-good industries. It applies just as much to someone running a digital product store, a SaaS company, or a financial planning firm. If you offer bookkeeping services, your Five Whys might start with: "I help small businesses manage their finances." Why is that important?

"So they can stay compliant and make informed decisions." And why is that important? "Because when they understand their numbers, they gain clarity and control." Again — why does that matter? "Because clarity builds confidence, and confidence drives business growth." One layer deeper? "Because thriving businesses support families and build strong communities." That's the shift. From spreadsheets to sustainability. From numbers to impact.

The beauty of the Five Whys is that it reconnects you with *meaning*. It moves you from offering a service to delivering a promise. And when you discover that promise, your messaging becomes magnetic. People don't just hear what you do — they *feel* why it matters.

This is especially critical when building your own media platforms. When you're not relying on the viral lottery of social media, every word has to work harder. It has to *carry weight*. Your content must reflect the *why* that drives you — because that's what creates resonance. That's what builds trust. People can spot fluff from a mile away. But when your words are backed by purpose, they hit differently. They land deeper.

The Five Whys isn't a one-time activity either. It's a practice — a compass you return to often. As your business grows, your goals may change, but your "why" remains the anchor. When things feel chaotic or confusing, when you're unsure what to write or offer next, go back to the Five Whys. Let them center you. Let them strip away the clutter.

So, take the time to go through this process. Don't rush it. Journal it out. Talk it through with someone you trust. Sit with the discomfort. Dig into the tension. Because when you finally hit that fifth "why," something opens. The surface-level answers give way to something sacred — the real reason you're here, doing what you do.

And that clarity? That's the fuel that will carry you through the hard seasons. That's the clarity your audience can feel. That's what makes you unforgettable. Absolutely.

## Simplify Your Message: Speak Clearly, Be Understood Quickly

Once you've uncovered the deep purpose behind your business — your why — the temptation is to hold onto it like a sacred artifact. And while that meaning is important to *you*, your audience doesn't need to hear the whole journey in one breath. They need something they can remember. Something they can repeat. Something they can feel in a sentence or two.

This is where so many brilliant business owners get stuck. They have a powerful story, a compelling offer, and years of lived experience… but when it comes time to share it with the world, the message is too long, too complex, or too vague. So it gets lost. And when a message gets lost, so does the opportunity.

Here's the truth: if your audience has to work hard to understand what you do, they'll move on. Not because they don't care but because their brain is already overloaded. In a world flooded with messages, clarity is kindness. Simplicity is service.

Think about some of the most iconic brands in the world. Nike doesn't talk about biomechanics, optimal heart rates, or fabric blends. They say, *Just do it.* Three words. But those words carry weight because of the brand's consistency, values, and story. It's not the words alone — it's the clarity behind them.

That same principle applies to your business.

Let's revisit the hair salon example. Imagine the internal purpose you uncovered through the Five Whys: "We empower self-confidence and happiness in our clients." That's meaningful — but a bit long for a Facebook bio or an Instagram caption. So you distill it. You simplify it without losing the heart. Maybe you land on:

*"Helping you look great and feel even better."*

Or:

*"Find the version of you that lights up the room."*

It's not about dumbing things down — it's about boiling things down to their emotional essence. When someone reads your tagline or hears your pitch, they should feel a spark of recognition. It should feel like you're speaking their language.

And speaking their language matters more than you might think.

Let's take a quick detour back to something we touched on earlier: speaking in a way your audience can actually hear. Remember the moment when I asked, *If I spoke to you in Shona, my native tongue, would you understand me?* The answer, of course, is no. And yet, that's what most business owners do — they speak in industry jargon, overcomplicate their offer, and unintentionally alienate the very people they're trying to help. Instead of saying, *"We offer advanced digital automation optimization systems,"* try something like, *"We help small business owners save hours a week by putting repetitive tasks on autopilot."* Same result. Different message. One speaks to the brain; the other speaks to the life someone wants to live.

So here's your invitation: simplify without watering down. Strip the message down to what matters. Ask yourself:

- What does my audience *really* want?

- What are the fewest, clearest words I can use to describe it?

- Does this message make someone say, *"That's me. That's what I need."*

You're not trying to impress your peers. You're trying to *reach your people.*

And once you do that, magic starts to happen. The conversations get easier. The content flows more naturally. Your audience starts using *your* words when they describe what they're going through — because you've spoken it better than they could. That's when you know you've struck gold.

Another way to pressure-test your message is to ask: *Can someone else repeat it on my behalf — and get it right?* If not, simplify again. If someone can't tell their friend what you do or forward your email and say, "This is the person I was telling you about," then you're making it too hard.

And what makes this so empowering is that everything else gets easier once your message is clear. Your email subjects, landing pages, webinar titles, and podcast intros —all draw from the same well. You're no longer reinventing the wheel with every piece of content. You're repeating what matters and deepening it over time.

This is how you become unforgettable — not by being louder, but by being consistent.

Remember, clarity isn't about saying everything. It's about saying the *right thing* at the *right time*, in the *right way*. And if you can master that — if you can say what needs to be said without needing a paragraph to say it — your business becomes a lighthouse. Clear. Steady. Seen.

# The Math of Engagement: How to Stay Top of Mind

Let's shift from mindset to mechanics.

You now understand the value of showing up before you sell. You know trust takes time and that each touchpoint matters. But how do you stay *at the top of your mind* in a world where everyone is swiping, scrolling, skipping, and skimming?

You do it by being *deliberate*. You do it by doing the math.

Here's what we've built at Livelong Digital — and why.

We created an email nurture sequence that spans **10 years**. Yes, ten. That's not a typo. And no, it's not because we expect someone to hang on every word of every message for a decade. It's because we understand the long game. If someone enters our ecosystem today, we want them to feel supported not just this week but six months from now, three years from now, even if they're not ready to buy until year five.

Now, that might sound overwhelming at first — but let's break it down.

A year has **52 weeks**. If you send an email every **three days**, you deliver roughly 100–120 emails yearly. Multiply that over 10 years, and you've got a nurture sequence with just over **1,000 pieces of content**. That's the foundation of a relationship. That's trust built drip by drip, story by story, insight by insight.

And before you think, *"I could never write that much,"* pause and reflect: you don't need to write all of it today. But what if you started thinking in terms of longevity? What if every piece of content you wrote wasn't just for this week's campaign but part of a library — a vault of value that future customers could tap into at any time?

That's how you future-proof your business.

When you're not chasing attention — but *earning loyalty*.

Our sequence is rooted in five pillars.

Every few emails, we rotate between these key questions:

1. **Here's what I've got** – what we offer.
2. **Here's what it will do for you** – the result it creates.
3. **Here's how it works** – a clear path or process.
4. **Here's what to do next** – a soft call to action.
5. **Here's why it's safe/smart** – the reassurance they didn't know they needed.

With these five lenses, we're always either educating, inspiring, affirming, or inviting. Every email isn't about a hard pitch — it's about showing up with something useful. And in the process, we train our audience to expect *value* when they see our name in their inbox. We become familiar. Trusted. Known.

And that's the key. Because the *top of the mind* is the *tip of the tongue*. People talk about what they think about. They recommend the brands they remember. So if you're the one showing up consistently and authentically, you're the one they'll mention when someone asks, *"Hey, do you know anyone who does this?"*

It's not flashy. But it works.

And that brings us to another powerful truth: **people want to be led**. They don't want to be spammed. They don't want to be stalked. But they *do* want to be guided. Gently. Intelligently. With empathy and insight.

That's your job. To be the guide. Not the hero. Not the hype machine. Just the one who shows up, day after day, offering direction.

And here's the beautiful part: once you do this enough — once you've built a sequence, a system, and a rhythm — you stop chasing leads. You start *filtering* them. You stop cold-pitching. You start *warming* them. Your marketing becomes more like matchmaking. The right people recognize themselves in your content. The wrong ones quietly move on. And that's okay. That's exactly how it should be.

Because in this world of overexposure, people don't need more content. They need *connection*. They don't need more pitches. They need *permission* to believe. To hope. To try again. And if you're the one who's been walking with them along the way — if you've earned their attention without demanding it — then when the time comes, they'll say what we've heard countless clients say:

*"I don't know why, but I just felt like you were the one I could trust."*

That's the reward of doing the math. Of thinking beyond the next launch. Of caring enough to plan ten years ahead.

So, here's your invitation: start building your own nurture sequence. It doesn't have to be perfect. It doesn't have to be long. It just has to be **honest, consistent**, and **relevant**. Start with three emails. Then make it ten. Then twenty. And before you know it, you've got an engine — a slow-burning fire that keeps your business warm through every season.

Here's what we've learned: when you engage with empathy, educate with clarity, and stay consistent — *you win trust by default.*

And trust, in the end, is what builds legacy.

# Belonging, Reassurance, and Value in Uncertain Times

The world is loud right now.

The economy is unpredictable. Social media platforms are shifting daily. Algorithms are tightening their grip. And your audience — real people with real lives — are navigating this storm just like you are. They're overwhelmed, distracted, and unsure of who to trust. And yet, they're still scrolling, still searching, still hoping someone will say something that helps them feel seen, heard, and safe.

This is your opportunity.

More than ever, people are craving **belonging**. Not just a good product. Not just a shiny offer. They want to feel like they matter. Like someone understands what they're going through. Like they're not alone in the chaos.

If you can offer that — through your words, stories, systems, and follow-up — you'll stand out without even trying to be flashy. Because the truth is, most people don't want a hero. They want a **guide**. Someone they can trust to walk with them. Someone who says, "I've been there too — and here's what I've learned."

In times of uncertainty, reassurance becomes a currency of its own. And this doesn't mean overpromising or sugarcoating reality. It means **communicating clearly**. It means showing up when others disappear. It means being generous with your wisdom, perspective, and attention — even when you're not selling anything.

That's what builds brand equity — not just clicks.

Think about it this way: if someone stumbles across your brand today and they're in survival mode — emotionally, financially, or mentally — they're not going to buy. But if you've built a system that *keeps speaking to them* even when they're silent, they will remember you when they're ready. And when they do, you'll already be in their world — not as a stranger, but as a trusted voice who was present when others weren't.

This is what we mean when we say **"own your media."** It is not just the technical side of it — the podcast, the blog, and the email list. But owning the *relationship*. Owning the follow-through. Owning your voice in a way that doesn't just seek attention but creates connection.

And to do that, you need to speak to three core emotional needs your audience carries — even if they never say them out loud:

**1.    The need to belong**

They want to feel like they're not the only ones struggling. Your stories, your transparency, your tone — all of that helps them feel included, not isolated.

## 2.     The need for reassurance

They want to know it's okay to be where they are and that their dreams are still valid. That someone out there believes in them.

## 3.     The need for value

Not just entertainment or noise but real, practical help. Quick wins. Fresh insight. Tangible outcomes. That's how trust is built.

Your brand becomes more than a business if you can consistently meet these needs — especially during uncertain times. It becomes a *safe space*. And people return to safe spaces. And here's what most people miss: reassurance isn't about grand gestures. It's about the small, consistent signals you send through your messaging. It's the friendly tone in your weekly emails. The thoughtful caption under your post. The way your landing page copy speaks to fears without exploiting them. The way you highlight wins without ignoring the hard parts.

When you do this well, your brand starts to feel like a friend — not a pitch. And when people feel emotionally

safe with your brand, they become not just customers...
but advocates.

They refer.

They reengage.

They remember.

And that kind of loyalty doesn't come from discounts
or flash sales. It comes from *depth*.

So don't underestimate the power of showing up
with calm, steady energy in a chaotic world. You don't
need to be everywhere. You don't need to go viral. You
just need to show up in the right way, for the right
people, with the right message — over and over again.

That's what makes your media *yours*. Not just because
it lives on your platform but because it reflects your
values. Your consistency. Your care.

And in a world of quick fixes and empty noise, that
care is exactly what people are looking for.

## The Checklist for Connection: Who, What, Where, When, and How

Now that we've explored what it means to build trust
and create emotional safety in your marketing, it's time to
ground that intention in something practical. Because
clarity isn't just about *what* you say — it's about *how*, *when*,
and *to whom* you say it.

That's where this checklist comes in.

Think of this as your compass — a simple yet powerful filter through which you can run all your content and communication. It doesn't matter whether you're writing an email, planning a podcast, or launching a new offer. If you don't check all five of these boxes, chances are you'll miss the mark.

Let's break them down:

## Who: Who's Speaking and Who's Listening?

Every message begins with *who*. Who are *you* in the eyes of your audience? Are you showing up as a relatable guide or as a disconnected expert? Are you positioning yourself as someone who truly understands their world or as someone speaking from a distance? Now ask: Who are *they*? Not everyone in your audience is the same. You may have early-stage clients, seasoned professionals, or hesitant browsers. Each one has different fears, desires, and levels of readiness. So, tailor your tone and language accordingly.

And remember: people listen when they feel like the message is **just for them**. If you're speaking in generalities, you're likely missing the emotional nuance that makes someone feel seen.

If I walked up to you and started speaking in Shona — my native language — without context, you'd likely stare blankly. Not because you're not intelligent, but because I didn't speak in a language you understand. That's what most online business owners do. They speak in *their* language, not their audience's. And then they wonder why no one's listening.

## What: What Are You Actually Offering?

Now that you've got the right people's attention, ask yourself: what exactly are you putting on the table?

Is it a product? A promise? A possibility?

Here's where clarity often falls apart. Business owners get so caught up in their features and jargon that they forget the one thing customers actually care about: **results**. What transformation are you offering? What will change in someone's life or business after working with you? What's the *outcome*?

Your audience isn't looking to fill their calendar with more commitments. They're looking for freedom, peace, solutions, confidence. So when they read about your offer, it needs to make them feel like *that's exactly what they've been looking for*.

And most importantly — make sure it's a message worth defending. If your client saw your offer on their credit card statement, would they fight to keep it? Or would it be the first thing they cancel next month?

That's the difference between a *cost* and a *conviction*. Build offers that hold their value.

## Where: Where Is This Message Being Seen or Heard?

Context matters.

A message that works beautifully in an email may fall flat on social media. A story that captivates your podcast listeners may not fit in a tweet.

The *platform* changes how your message is received.

So before you hit publish, ask: *Where is this showing up?* Is this a place where people multitask or are deeply focused? Are they likely to read long-form content, or are they just scrolling to kill time? Are they expecting depth... or entertainment? Don't try to make every platform serve the same purpose. Use each one strategically — but **anchor** them all in one place: your owned media.

Because your website, your blog, your email list — those are places where you can control the environment, the tone, and the experience. That's where your message can truly breathe.

## When: When Does This Message Arrive, and What State Are They In?

Timing is everything.

Think about your audience's daily life. Are they reading your email in the middle of a workday, skimming between Zoom calls? Are they checking their phone late at night, tired and distracted? Or maybe they're in a season of doubt, transition, or frustration.

You don't just need to know *who* they are — you need to know *where* they are mentally, emotionally, and physically when your message lands.

If someone is stressed out, a heavy pitch might feel like pressure. But a thoughtful insight or a relatable story could land just right. If they're in a moment of curiosity or openness, a bold invitation might be exactly what they need.

So, consider the rhythm of your content. Are you always "asking," or are you also "affirming"? Are you hitting send just to stay on schedule, or are you tuning in to where your audience actually is?

Think Goldilocks. Not too soon. Not too late. *Just right.*

## How: What Format, Tone, and Delivery Are You Using?

Finally, we come to the *how*.

How are you showing up — visually, vocally, energetically?

Is your tone warm and welcoming? Confident but not arrogant? Is your language accessible? Are your visuals supporting the message or distracting from it?

And beyond tone — how are you delivering your message? Is it a casual email, a formal launch, a video walkthrough, or a carousel on Instagram?

The format you choose sends its own message. A 45-minute video signals depth. A five-sentence email signals quick value. A handwritten note in the mail? That says care.

So ask yourself: *Does the format match the intention?* Is it helping the message land or getting in the way?

Because here's the hard truth: you can have the perfect audience, offer, and message — and still miss the mark if your format and tone are off.

Together, these five questions — Who, What, Where, When, and How — form the foundation of your communication strategy. They ensure that your message isn't just *sent* — it's *received*. That your words don't just float past your audience — they stick.

This is the art of alignment.

This is how brands become voices.

This is how messages become movements.

So, as you build out your own media ecosystem, return to these questions often. Let them guide your email copy, podcast outlines, video scripts, and sales pages. Don't just hit publish. Hit *home*.

Because when you connect on all five levels, you don't just sell — you serve.

And service, in the end, is what turns strangers into followers… and followers into fans.

## Your Media, Your Voice: The Value You Offer to the World.

By now, you've realized this isn't just about marketing. It's about meaning. You're not just building a content calendar — you're building a **connection engine**. You're not just creating posts — you're building a platform where your voice has weight, your message becomes medicine, and your presence becomes *the place people return to* for clarity, strength, and hope.

Owning your media means owning your voice. And that voice — your voice — carries value.

Let's be real for a moment. There are thousands of people doing what you do. Selling similar products. Offering similar services. Talking to the same market. But what makes your brand irreplaceable isn't the tools you use or the tactics you apply. It's **how you show up**. It's the *energy* behind your message. The stories you choose to tell. The sincerity in your tone. The quiet authority in your delivery. The consistency in your presence.

When people feel your heartbeat behind the brand, they don't just listen — they *lean in.*

That's the gift of building your own media. You're no longer confined to what the algorithm rewards. You're no longer chasing likes or fighting for fleeting attention. You're playing a different game — one of legacy, trust, and emotional resonance.

You get to speak directly to your audience on your terms and in your own time. You get to guide them through their fears, doubts, desires, and breakthroughs with the language *you* choose. With stories that *you* believe in. With content that doesn't expire after 24 hours.

You're not a prisoner to platforms. You're not a pawn in someone else's game.

You're a leader with something meaningful to say — and now, you have a place to say it.

But let's make this even more practical. Owning your media gives you three powerful outcomes — the kind that build *real* businesses, not just digital noise.

**1.    You protect your peace.**

When you build on your own platform, you're not scrambling every time a new update drops or an algorithm shifts. You're anchored. You're consistent. You're in control. This brings calm to your business and clarity to your actions. No more reactive chaos. Just a grounded strategy.

## 2. You attract the right people.

When your message is clear, and your delivery is steady, you naturally repel the wrong fit and resonate with those who are meant to work with you. You don't have to scream. You don't have to beg. You become a lighthouse — visible to the right ships, guiding them safely to shore.

## 3. You multiply your impact.

As your content lives on, your message spreads, and your nurture systems deepen relationships over time, you stop hustling for attention and expand your *influence*. You become known. Not just because you're loud — but because you're *true*. This is what we mean when we say your media is your ministry. It's not just a marketing channel — it's a container for your wisdom. A stage for your stories. A canvas for your purpose. And when done with intention, it's one of the most powerful gifts you can offer the world. So, as we wrap up this chapter, take a breath and remember this:

You don't have to go viral to be valuable.

You don't have to be everywhere to be effective.

You don't have to build fast — you just have to build faithfully. What you're doing matters. The way you show up matters. And the media you create today is planting seeds you'll harvest for years to come.

So, go back to your core message.

Clarify your voice.

Speak with honesty.

Serve with boldness.

And trust that those who are meant to hear you — *will*.

You've already begun. You're no longer just "doing marketing."

You're building something that lasts.

Let's keep going.

# Chapter 5: S.imply E.ducate O.thers

Take a moment and ask yourself — why do people really come to the internet?

It seems like a basic question, right? But too many business owners miss this entirely. They rush to create content, launch ads, or throw up another social post, all without stopping to ask what people are genuinely looking for when they go online. And when you don't understand why people come to the internet, how can you expect them to find you, trust you, buy from you, or refer others?

The truth is this: people come to the internet for just three reasons. Not five. Not ten. Just three.

*Entertainment.*

*Information.*

*Shopping.*

That's it. We call this the EIS framework. It may sound simple, but it's the bedrock of everything we're about to build. Think of your own habits — when you open your browser, unlock your phone, or refresh your feed, what are you usually doing? Maybe you're watching something funny to decompress after a long day. Maybe you're researching how to fix your leaky sink or comparing the best email marketing tools. Or maybe you're scrolling for something to buy — shoes, groceries, a birthday gift, a new course... So, let's bring this closer to home. If you're building a business in today's world, you must meet your audience exactly where they are — inside one of those three lanes. Because they didn't come online to find you. They came online for themselves.

And your job is to become part of their answer.

This chapter is where the rubber meets the road. In the previous chapters, we worked hard to define your market and shape your message. You now know who you're speaking to and what to say. But the next step — this step — is to figure out how you're going to reach them consistently. Not just once or twice, but in a reliable, repeatable way. Without depending on platforms that could change the rules at any moment.

This chapter is about owning your reach. It's about becoming the go-to voice in your niche without letting algorithms, policies, or random trends decide if you get heard. This chapter is where you shift from being a passive content creator to becoming a proactive distributor of your own message.

Because here's the truth — if you don't own the way your content is delivered, someone else does. And if someone else owns it, they can change, mute, or remove it.

That's not a strategy. That's a gamble.

You didn't come this far to leave your growth up to chance.

## Owning vs. Renting: Why Platform Ownership Matters

Let's talk about rented land.

You see, posting on platforms like Facebook, Instagram, TikTok, or even YouTube feels empowering... until it's not. It feels like you're building something — until one day, you realize you're building it on someone else's soil. And when they decide to move the fence, change the rules, or shut down the site, you're left stranded.

We've all heard the saying: "Don't build your house on rented land." But what does that mean in the online world?

This means that if your entire audience lives on Instagram, you don't own it. If your best content only exists in TikTok videos, you don't control it. If your email list is managed entirely by a platform that could go dark or block you, you're vulnerable.

That's the difference between renting and owning. Renting means you're at the mercy of others. Owning means you call the shots.

Let me paint the picture another way. Renting land is like setting up a lemonade stand on a busy street corner. You get foot traffic, sure. But you also get noise. Distractions. Competitors on every side. And worst of all? At any point, the landlord can come over and say, "Pack it up. You're done here."

Owning your land, on the other hand, means building your own store. It means people come to you — not because they were scrolling randomly, but because they know, trust, and want what you have. And once they step inside, the environment is yours to control. No random shutdowns. No shadow bans. No content filters. Just you, your brand, and your audience — uninterrupted.

I know what it's like to be on the wrong side of that divide. When I lost access to my Facebook account, I lost years of momentum. Not just content — connection. The real-time engagement, the comments, and the community are gone. And what hurt the most wasn't the data. It was the realization that I never really had a say in the first place.

That was the wake-up call. And that's why I'm telling you this now: don't wait for a crisis to start owning your platform. Start today.

So, what does ownership actually look like?

It starts with simple tools that give you full control:

Your **website** — your digital storefront, open 24/7, shaped entirely by your brand.

Your **email list** — your most intimate and reliable form of contact, immune to algorithms.

Your **podcast** — a personal, on-demand voice in your audience's earbuds.

Your **blog** — your evergreen knowledge base, searchable and shareable.

Your **online community** — whether it's a forum, a membership site, or a private group you host.

These are assets. Real, lasting digital assets. And when you build them, you don't just increase your visibility — you create freedom. Freedom to market without guesswork. Freedom to share without restrictions. Freedom to pivot, grow, and adapt without someone else holding the keys.

But there's one more piece to this: **distribution**.

Owning your media means nothing if you don't know how to distribute it. This is why understanding *how* your content gets seen, heard, and consumed is just as important as creating it. Distribution is what keeps the message moving — from your blog to your inbox to someone's morning stroll. It's the bridge between what you say and what your audience receives.

And here's the best part: when you own your platform, distribution becomes a system, not a mystery.

You're no longer wondering if the algorithm will "bless" your post. You're not crossing your fingers hoping people find your latest video. Instead, you're crafting intentional pathways that guide your audience from first touch to lifelong trust.

It's not just strategy. It's sovereignty.

It's your voice, delivered your way to your people — every single time.

So before we dive into the mechanics of media distribution and content formats, ask yourself this:

Am I ready to stop renting?

Am I ready to start building something I actually own?

Because if the answer is yes, what comes next will change everything.

## Understanding Your Media Modality: Voice, Writing, or Video

By now, you've done the deep work of understanding who you're speaking to and what your message should be. You've crafted your value proposition, defined your market, and started to create content that resonates. But another key element determines your success—how you deliver that message. This is where media modality comes in. Think of it as your personal communication superpower. Are you a speaker? A writer? Someone who comes alive on camera? Or maybe you've never even paused to consider it.

Most people, especially when starting out in business, fall into the trap of trying to be everywhere. They blog. They post on social media. They dabble in podcasting. They try to show up on YouTube or record courses. But in trying to do everything, they end up doing very little well. Worse, they burn out. So, instead of playing the "be-everywhere" game, it's time to pick a lane. One clear, focused modality that feels natural and enjoyable to you. That's where sustainability lives. And that's where your unique voice shines brightest.

Let's break it down. There are three primary media modalities you can focus on: voice, writing, and video. Each has its strengths, and none is inherently better than the other. The key is alignment—choosing what energizes you rather than what you think you "should" be doing.

If you're drawn to **voice**, you're in good company. Podcasts, webinars, interviews, and audio snippets fall under this category. Maybe you're the kind of person who loves explaining things out loud, thrives in conversation, or enjoys storytelling. Voice is intimate.

People feel like they're in the room with you. It's also portable—people can consume your message while jogging, driving, or washing dishes. Best of all, it doesn't require makeup, lighting, or a perfect camera setup. A quiet room and a decent mic can take you far. If talking lights you up and ideas come out of your mouth faster than your hands can type them, the voice might be your lane.

If, on the other hand, you find yourself pouring your heart into captions or jotting down ideas in the Notes app at 2 a.m., then **writing** may be your home base. Writing is powerful because it allows for depth. You can explain ideas thoroughly, build structured arguments, and create evergreen assets that serve your audience over time. Blogs, newsletters, whitepapers, ebooks, and even long-form social media posts all fall into this category. Writing also has the unique advantage of being highly indexable—Google loves it, and that helps your SEO in the long run. If you've got stories to tell or expertise to share, writing gives you the canvas.

Then there's **video**—an incredibly engaging blend of voice and presence. Video isn't just about being "on camera." It's about showing up in a way that connects visually and emotionally. If you're expressive, comfortable making eye contact with the lens, and not afraid to show your face, video allows for maximum connection. It's the fastest way to build rapport and trust. People get to see your mannerisms, your energy, and your authenticity. From YouTube videos and Instagram reels to live broadcasts and recorded courses, video covers a lot of ground. Of course, it also requires a bit more setup—camera, lighting, editing—but if it comes naturally, those technical bits become minor details.

Here's the secret: you don't need to master all three. In fact, you shouldn't. You just need to master one—and own it. That becomes your **anchor modality**. The place where you show up consistently. The format you can maintain even when life gets busy or unpredictable. Once you've mastered that modality, everything else becomes easier. You can repurpose that core piece of content into the others. A podcast episode can be transcribed into a blog. A blog can become a script for a video. A video can be sliced into reels or quoted in an email. But trying to do all three from the start? That's a recipe for exhaustion.

So here's what I want you to do: pause and reflect. Think about your natural tendencies. Are you a talker, a writer, or a performer? When you're communicating, what feels easy, even fun? Where do you feel energized rather than drained? Don't overthink it—your gut already knows the answer. Write down your dominant modality, then list a few ways you could consistently commit to showing up in that format. This clarity alone will help you cut through overwhelm and start building a distribution strategy that works for you—not against you.

## The Buyer's Journey and the Role of Distribution

Now that you've chosen your core modality, it's time to explore how to actually use it to move your audience from first contact to paying customers. Because let's face it: creating great content is one thing, but getting it in front of the right people—and guiding them toward a decision—is where the magic happens. This is where **distribution** and **the buyer's journey** come into play.

Every customer, consciously or not, goes through a decision-making process before purchasing. In marketing, we often describe this as the **AIDA** framework: Awareness → Interest → Desire → Action. Each stage requires a different kind of message and a different delivery method. If you show up with a sales pitch at the Awareness stage, you'll scare people away. You'll miss your chance if you keep talking about problems and solutions when they're ready to buy. Your job is to meet your audience where they are and gently guide them toward action.

Let's begin with **Awareness**. This is where people are just discovering you. They may not know they have a problem yet or may not be actively seeking a solution. Your content at this stage should be generous, engaging, and broadly appealing. This is where blog posts, podcast episodes, YouTube videos, or social media posts play a critical role. You're not selling here—you're showing up, creating visibility, and offering insight. This is how people stumble upon you and think, "Hey, this person gets it."

Once people are aware of you, they move into the **Interest** phase. Now they're curious. They've heard your voice, read your words, or watched your videos. They like your vibe. They're wondering, "What else do they offer?" This is the perfect time to introduce a **lead magnet**—a free resource that gives value in exchange for their email. Think of this as the virtual handshake. A checklist, a free training, a mini-course, or an exclusive guide. This is also where your **email list** becomes invaluable. You begin nurturing the relationship. You start building familiarity and trust through automated emails, thoughtful content, and relevant insights.

Then comes **Desire**. At this stage, your audience knows they need what you offer. They trust you, but they're looking for proof. This is where testimonials, case studies, success stories, and behind-the-scenes content matter. You want to show the transformation—real people, real results, real change. This is also the time to share your methods, your philosophy, and the unique value you bring. Desire builds when people can visualize themselves succeeding with your help.

Finally, we arrive at **Action**. This is the moment of decision. Your call to action should be clear, simple, and confident. Whether it's booking a call, purchasing a product, or enrolling in a program, make it easy for people to take the next step. No friction. No confusion. Just a seamless transition from thinking to doing. And because you've owned the distribution all along—through your website, podcast, blog, and email—they've arrived at this point because of your ecosystem, not some unpredictable algorithm.

Understanding the buyer's journey isn't just about structure—it's about empathy. It's recognizing that your audience is on a path, and your job is to walk with them. To lead with trust. To show up consistently. And ensure that your content aligns with where they are—not where you wish they were.

So, how does this tie back to owning your media?

Simple. When you own your media—your platform, your content, your distribution—you control the journey. You're not hoping someone sees your post in a sea of noise. You're not crossing your fingers that your video goes viral. You're building a clear, strategic, value-driven system that delivers the right message to the right person at the right time.

The truth is your audience wants to trust someone. They're looking for guidance. They're looking for consistency. They're looking for results. And if you build your distribution channels to support each stage of their journey, you become the natural choice.

It starts with picking your modality. It grows with thoughtful, aligned content. And it blossoms when you own your ecosystem—from the first blog post to the final conversion.

In the next section, we'll take this even further by helping you design a distribution strategy that fits your strengths and works in the real world—week after week, month after month. But for now, reflect on what you've just read.

What content will you create to build Awareness?

What lead magnet will you offer to spark Interest?

What stories will you tell to inspire Desire?

And what simple step will you ask them to take when they're ready for Action?

Because when your content meets them at every stage—and when you own that entire journey—you stop chasing clients. They start showing up at your door, ready to work with you.

That's the power of owned distribution. And that's how you build a business that lasts.

## The Lead Magnet and Welcome Sequence

By now, you've identified your ideal audience, clarified your message, and selected the medium that aligns with your strengths. You've learned to respect the buyer's journey and show up intentionally through every stage. But how do you turn passive readers, listeners, or viewers into engaged community members? The answer lies in one of the most foundational yet overlooked pieces of any marketing system: the lead magnet.

Let's simplify what a lead magnet really is. At its core, a lead magnet is a small gift. It's a moment of value offered in exchange for trust. You're saying, "Let me help you with something small so you can see I'm the person to help with something big." It's that first handshake, the first cup of coffee in a relationship you hope will last a long time.

But it's more than just a freebie. A good lead magnet is intentional, precise, and deeply aligned with your audience's core problem. It should solve a real pain point or offer a quick win, giving your audience a sense of progress. When done right, it becomes a filter that separates the mildly curious from the genuinely interested.

There are countless types of lead magnets, and your choice should match both your content style and your audience's preferences. For example, if you're a coach working with overwhelmed entrepreneurs, a simple **Productivity Checklist** might give them a sense of control. If you're a fitness expert, a short **eBook on Meal Prep for Busy Professionals** could meet your audience where they are. Perhaps you're in the personal development space—a **5-day email Course** on building better habits might be the ideal entry point. Let's not forget the power of **quizzes**. They're engaging and interactive and provide insight to you and your audience. A coach helping people find their passion might create a quiz titled "What's Your Entrepreneurial Archetype?" The participant gets clarity, and you get data. That's a win-win.

But the lead magnet is just the beginning. What happens next determines whether the relationship grows or fizzles out. This is where the **welcome sequence** comes into play. Think of it as your digital orientation program. You've invited someone into your world—now it's your job to show them around.

An effective welcome sequence doesn't need to be complicated. In fact, the simpler, the better. At Livelong Digital, we recommend a **three-part email sequence** designed to build familiarity, deliver value, and establish trust. Let's break it down:

## Email 1: Know You

The first email should be warm, inviting, and authentic. Introduce yourself—not just your title or your credentials, but your story. Why do you do what you do? What challenges have you overcome? What do you stand for? People don't connect with brands; they connect with people. This is your chance to be human and real and set the tone for a relationship rooted in trust.

## Email 2: Like You

Now that your reader knows a little about you, it's time to give them something of value. This could be an insightful blog post, a video that explains a key concept, or a free tool that builds on the lead magnet they just downloaded. Your goal here is to be helpful, not salesy. Show them that your content is more than fluff—it's relevant, practical, and created with them in mind.

## Email 3: Trust You

Finally, establish credibility. Share a story of transformation—either your own or a client's. Include a testimonial or a before-and-after case study. If you have social proof, this is the time to use it. And if it feels natural, introduce a low-barrier offer. It's not a hard sell—just an invitation to take the next step. Perhaps a free discovery call, an invite to a webinar, or a special offer on a starter program.

This three-part sequence is deceptively simple but incredibly powerful. It introduces you. It provides value. It shows results. Most importantly, it does all this while nurturing trust step by step, email by email.

What's remarkable about this system is how it runs in the background. Once set up, it works for you 24/7. Someone could download your lead magnet at 2 a.m.; by sunrise, they've met you, learned from you, and begun to see you as someone they can trust. This is the magic of owning your media: you're no longer at the mercy of social platforms or algorithms. You're building a system that nurtures, informs, and converts—quietly, consistently, and authentically.

## Personal Story: From Facebook Lives to Owning the Conversation

If you've followed the story so far, you know that everything I've written in this book didn't come from theory. It came from hard-earned experience—specifically, the day I lost access to the Facebook platform I had poured my soul into for years.

Every weekday at 2 p.m. AEST, I'd go live without fail. My audience knew to tune in. We had built a rhythm—interactive sessions, live feedback, and real-time problem-solving.

It wasn't just marketing; it was community. But one afternoon, everything changed. I logged in to go live, and my account was gone. No warning. No explanation. No appeal process that made sense. I was gutted. My content—dozens of videos and hours of teaching was unreachable. But more than that, my audience was gone. The very people I had worked so hard to connect with were now out of reach, and I had no way to tell them what had happened or where I had gone. I sat in my office, staring at my mic, unsure of what to do next.

At first, I did what most people do in moments of loss—I ranted. I recorded angry episodes into that microphone, venting into the void about what had just happened. Twelve episodes, all heat, and heartbreak. And then something shifted. I realized I could keep yelling at Zuckerberg or do something better—I could own the conversation.

So, I started over. This time, not on Facebook. I started recording intentional podcast episodes. I created thoughtful content that spoke to my ideal audience, not the algorithm. I didn't need to chase likes, shares, or watch time. I needed to serve. And with each episode, I found clarity—not just about what I wanted to say, but how I wanted to show up.

Fifteen episodes in, I got my first response. A listener messaged me: "I couldn't find you on Facebook, but I found you on Spotify. I've missed hearing your voice." That message changed everything. I realized I wasn't shouting into the void—I was rebuilding a bridge. One episode at a time, I was reconnecting with the people who mattered.

I started adding links in the show notes. Resources. Free downloads. Lead magnets. Suddenly, people weren't just listening—they were opting in. I began collecting emails, not just followers. My content wasn't disappearing into a feed; it was being received, saved, and responded to. I had gone from chasing attention to **owning the conversation**.

That's the gift of owned media. It starts humbly—with a single episode, a single blog post, and a single opt-in form. But over time, it builds momentum. You become searchable. You become shareable. And you become trusted—not because a platform said you were valuable, but because you showed up consistently with real solutions.

Today, the podcast has over 300 episodes, organized into seasons that align with the stages of my audience's journey. From beginner to advanced, each listener can find the episode that meets them exactly where they are. That's what I want for you. You don't need to start big. You just need to start. Start with what you have. Start from where you are. And then scale intentionally.

That's what I did. I recorded one episode, then two, then ten. I listened to what people asked for. I responded. I adapted. I created resources based on feedback. And slowly, I built a media ecosystem that worked without relying on a social media platform that could vanish overnight. If there's one takeaway from this story, it's this: when you own the means of communication, you never lose the conversation. That's the power of owned media. And that's what I hope you'll embrace in your own business.

You don't need perfect lighting or a million followers. You need a voice, a message, and a system. And if you've read this far, you already have the first two. The rest can be built.

So, what will your next step be? A checklist? A three-part email sequence? A single podcast episode? Start there. Start with one moment of clarity, one asset that brings someone into your world. Because once you start owning your media, you stop waiting for permission. You stop hoping the algorithm sees you. You become the signal in a sea of noise.

And that, my friend, is how you build not just a business—but a legacy.

## Designing a Buyer-Focused Content Journey

Once you've laid the groundwork with a lead magnet and a welcome sequence, the next step is to guide your potential customers along a content journey that meets them where they are—and gently walks them toward where they want to be. This isn't about pushing them into a purchase; it's about supporting them at every stage of their thinking, researching, and decision-making process. A buyer-focused content journey is like building a trail in the forest: it's lit, well-marked, and easy to follow. Your job is to guide, not to chase.

You might remember in earlier chapters when we talked about your ideal customer and the importance of understanding their internal struggles, fears, and dreams. Well, this is where all that hard work pays off. Because when you know what your customers are experiencing—and what future they're hoping for—you can reverse-engineer your content to serve that exact transformation.

Start by mapping out the full lifecycle of a potential customer. Think about the moment before they even know you exist. What questions are they asking? What pain are they Googling solutions for? This is the **Awareness Stage**. Your goal here is to help them name their problem. You're not selling. You're not promoting. You're offering clarity. Articles like "7 Signs Your

Coaching Isn't Working" or podcast episodes like "Feeling Stuck? Here's What That Really Means" are perfect examples of top-of-funnel content that builds trust without asking for anything in return.

Then, as they begin to explore potential solutions, they move into the **Interest Stage**. Here, they're actively looking for answers, comparing approaches, and starting to evaluate who might be able to help them. This is where your how-to content, webinars, and case studies shine. You might offer them a downloadable guide or invite them to a free masterclass. The goal here is to show them that not only do you understand the problem—they can start solving it with your help.

Next comes **Desire**. At this point, they're beginning to trust you. They've seen your name in their inbox. They've read your posts or listened to your podcast. They're asking: "Could this be the person who helps me finally figure this out?" This is your moment to share testimonials, behind-the-scenes glimpses of your process, and value-packed content that shows them what's possible when they work with you. Remember, you're not just selling your service—you're offering them a vision of who they could become.

And finally, we arrive at the **Action Stage**. This is when the potential client is ready to make a decision. Your job now is to remove friction and make the next step as easy as possible. Whether it's a clear "Schedule a Free Call" button, a checkout page for your product, or a limited-time invitation to your group program, clarity and simplicity are essential. This is not the time to overcomplicate. At this stage, your message should be focused, your offer obvious, and your invitation confident.

What's powerful about this journey is that it doesn't need to be perfect from day one. Many business owners wait far too long to create this kind of experience because they believe it has to be flawless. But remember what we said earlier: Start with what you have. Refine as you go. The important thing is to begin crafting a series of touchpoints that guide your potential client closer to you, piece by piece.

At Livelong Digital, we often compare this journey to a plane flight. Think of your business as an airline. The client's first encounter with you is when they're scanning options online—they're comparing routes, looking at costs, and wondering which airline is the safest bet. Once they choose to fly with you (opt-in), your welcome sequence is the gate agent greeting them, checking their ticket, and welcoming them aboard. From there, your content is the in-flight experience: the service, the comfort, the reassurance. By the time the plane lands, your client feels like they've been taken care of. They're ready to fly with you again, and I'll tell their friends about it, too.

The goal of designing this kind of buyer-focused journey is not just to close more sales. It's to create a business that feels aligned, sustainable, and human. No more chasing. No more guessing. Clear, consistent communication with the people already looking for what you offer.

## Repurposing and Distribution Strategy

Now that you've developed a lead magnet, a welcome sequence, and a content journey that aligns with your buyer's mindset, let's talk about one of the most powerful levers in your marketing toolbox: repurposing and distribution. If content is your voice, distribution is your microphone. And repurposing? That's the amplifier.

Here's the truth: You don't need to create more content. You need to use your content better.

The reason most coaches and entrepreneurs feel overwhelmed by content is that they believe they have to be everywhere, all the time, with something new to say. But that's not sustainable, and more importantly—it's not strategic. You're not here to be a full-time content creator. You're here to run a business. So, the key is to work smarter, not harder. And that starts with repurposing.

Repurposing means taking one piece of content and spinning it into multiple formats across different platforms. Let's say you've written a blog post titled "5 Mistakes New Coaches Make in Their First Year." That single article can become:

A podcast episode where you talk through the five mistakes with added commentary.

Five social media posts, each focusing on one mistake.

A downloadable checklist: "Are You Making These Mistakes?"

A short reel or video clip summarizing the list.

An email to your list with a personal story related to one of the points.

One idea. Five to ten outputs. That's the power of repurposing.

And here's where it gets even better: when you know what your preferred content modality is (voice, writing, or video), you can build your strategy around it. For example, record your episode first if you're naturally great at podcasting. Then, transcribe it into a blog post. Pull quotes for your social media. Create a one-minute teaser video. That's how you turn a single 30-minute effort into a week's worth of content.

Now, let's shift to **distribution**. Repurposing gives you more content. Distribution ensures that content is seen, heard, and engaged with. If repurposing is about making your ideas travel further, distribution is about choosing the right roads for them to travel on.

Start by identifying your **primary distribution channel**—the one place where your ideal clients hang out. This could be LinkedIn, Instagram, YouTube, Substack, your email list, or even a private Facebook group. The key is to pick one platform and go deep, not wide. Quality engagement on one platform always beats lukewarm attention on five. Let's say your audience is primarily on LinkedIn. Great. Your blog post becomes a long-form post. Your checklist becomes a downloadable document you share in the comments. Your podcast becomes an audio clip embedded in a LinkedIn article. By staying focused, you develop consistency and presence—and your audience begins to recognize you as a valuable voice in their space.

Next, choose **secondary distribution channels** to extend your reach. This could include syndicating your blog on Medium, sharing clips on Instagram Stories, or republishing content via newsletters or strategic partnerships. However, the purpose of these channels is to lead people back to your core platform, where deeper conversation and conversion happen.

This is where owning your media truly becomes liberating. Because you no longer rely on the algorithm to do the heavy lifting. You've created an ecosystem: a central home (your website, podcast, or email list) and a series of bridges that guide people to it. This is how you future-proof your business. This is how you create a system that generates results long after you hit publish.

At Livelong Digital, we often use what we call the **Core + Spokes Model**. Your core is your main content asset—typically your podcast, YouTube channel, or blog. The spokes are the smaller, bite-sized pieces of content (social posts, quotes, stories, snippets) that extend from that core and bring people back to it. It's like having a wheel that keeps spinning—with the core holding it all together.

But here's the part most people miss: repurposing and distribution are not just about efficiency. They're about **reinforcement**. When your audience sees your message in multiple formats on multiple platforms, it builds trust. It increases memorability. It gives the impression that you're everywhere—even if you only spent one hour a week creating content.

The final layer of this strategy is **consistency**. None of this works if you show up once and disappear for a month. Consistency doesn't mean posting every day. It means showing up at a pace you can maintain. Weekly, bi-weekly, even monthly—just pick a rhythm and stick with it. You're training your audience to expect value from you. And when you deliver consistently, you become a reliable voice in their world.

So here's your challenge: look at your last piece of content and ask yourself—how many different ways could I repurpose this? Where else could I distribute it? What format would make it easier for my audience to consume? These questions are not just tactical. They're transformational because they shift you from being a content producer to being a media strategist.

And that's exactly what you are now becoming.

You're no longer just building a business. You're building a media company—one piece of content, one repurposed asset, one distributed message at a time. You are designing a journey that honors your audience and amplifies your voice.

And the best part? You're doing it on your own terms.

## Building a Long-Term Content System That Works While You Sleep

By now, you've realized that creating content isn't about showing up randomly or chasing trends. It's about building a system—a living, breathing-controlled machine that works while you sleep. Imagine waking up to emails from people thanking you for your insight, discovering that someone binge-watched your YouTube series overnight, or seeing your lead magnet downloaded by a complete stranger who stumbled across one of your articles at 3 a.m. That is what happens when your content ecosystem is set up to work 24/7.

Let's be honest—most coaches, consultants, and creative entrepreneurs don't struggle with a lack of talent. They struggle with a lack of systems. They have valuable insights, real solutions, and genuine passion, but all of it stays scattered without a structure. Inconsistent content leads to inconsistent results. That's where your long-term system comes in: to take the pressure off and keep the momentum going, even when life gets in the way.

So, what does a system like this actually look like? At its core, it's made up of three parts: your primary content engine, your repurposing framework, and your automation setup.

Your **primary content engine** is the heart of your message. This could be your podcast, weekly blog, YouTube series, or newsletter. It's the one format you show up for consistently, regardless of what else is happening online. If everything else fell away—social media, algorithms, platforms—this would remain. Think of it as your lighthouse, your anchor, your home base.

Then comes your **repurposing framework**—the bridge between your long-form content and your wider audience.

This is where you take that one blog post or podcast episode and spin it into multiple pieces. You might turn quotes into Instagram posts, record a 1-minute video summary, or send out a related email. It's not about doing more—it's about doing smarter. The beauty of repurposing is that once your process is in place, it doesn't require more creativity, just consistency. And finally, you have your **automation setup**. This includes scheduling tools, evergreen nurture sequences, and onboarding flows. These systems keep your content moving through the pipeline, guiding your audience from first contact to warm lead to raving fan. Automation isn't about removing the human touch; it's about freeing your time so you can be more present where it matters most.

To make this system work, you need to **zoom out** and see the bigger picture. Each piece of content should fit somewhere in your customer's journey. Your top-of-funnel content should attract strangers and help them identify their pain. Your middle-of-funnel content should deepen the connection and demonstrate your ability to help. Your bottom-of-funnel content should create clarity, confidence, and ease around the decision to work with you.

This is the invisible magic of a long-term content system. It replaces randomness with rhythm. It trades burnout for balance. And over time, it builds the kind of brand that people don't just recognize—they rely on. Think of your content system as a garden. You plant seeds (your blogs, podcasts, or videos), water them (through repurposing and promotion), and eventually grow a field of trust. And trust, as you've heard before, is the currency of conversion. Here's a quick tip: block one day each month to assess your ecosystem. Ask yourself: Is my content aligned with my audience's current needs? Are my nurture sequences still relevant? Am I creating from a place of joy or pressure? Don't be afraid to refine and update your system. The goal is not perfection; it's progression.

When done right, your content system becomes your most reliable employee. It never takes a vacation. It doesn't get sick. It works on weekends. And it introduces you to new people day after day—people who are already pre-qualified, primed, and curious about what you have to offer.

Remember this: building a content system is not a side project—it is the business. Marketing is not something you do after you've created your offer. It's how your offer finds its people. And if you build your system with care, it will not only generate leads—it will generate legacy.

## Choosing Your Core Content Channel and Sticking With It

Now that we've talked about the importance of a long-term content system, let's talk about the foundation of that system: choosing your core content channel. This decision is more important than it may seem at first glance. Because the truth is, when it comes to owning your media, consistency always beats complexity. And the best way to stay consistent is to play to your strengths. Here's what most people do wrong: they try to be everywhere. One day, they're on TikTok; the next, they're blogging; the next, they're starting a YouTube channel they'll abandon in two weeks. The result? Scattered attention, burnout, and a brand that feels confusing and inconsistent. The smarter move? Pick one core content channel—and go all in.

Whatever you choose, make sure it's something you can commit to weekly, bi-weekly, or monthly—without dreading it. If it doesn't energize you, you won't stick with it. And if you don't stick with it, it doesn't matter how brilliant your content is. It will get buried under inconsistency.

Think of your core content channel as your **flagship show**—the one place where your audience knows they can find your best thinking, your most helpful ideas, and your most authentic voice. Everything else—social media posts, emails, snippets—should flow from this source. When you have a clear home base for your message, you create familiarity. And familiarity breeds trust.

Now, here's the key: your core channel doesn't need to be massive. It doesn't need to go viral. It doesn't even need to have a huge audience. It just needs to be consistent. Because the person who finds you at the right time—when they're searching, hurting, or stuck—isn't looking for the biggest creator. They're looking for someone who understands.

Let me give you a practical example from my own business. After losing access to Facebook Lives, I didn't scramble to replace it with 10 different strategies. I chose one: a podcast. That podcast became my home base. From there, I built a content ecosystem that fed everything else—my email list, my blog, and my client conversations. And because I focused, I could grow. And because I grew, I could lead.

Choosing your core content channel also gives you a powerful filter for your time and energy. When opportunities come up—guest interviews, social collaborations, launches—you can ask yourself: Does this support or distract from my core channel? It helps you say no with confidence and say yes with clarity.

Of course, over time, your content journey may evolve. You might start with a blog and eventually launch a podcast. Or begin with YouTube and later transition into a paid newsletter. That's okay. What matters most is that you build a rhythm you can grow into, not a routine you burn out from.

Let's take a moment here to visualize your audience. Picture someone discovering your core content for the first time. Maybe they're on a morning walk, earbuds in, listening to your podcast. Or maybe they've stumbled onto your blog late at night, eyes scanning your words with the quiet intensity of someone who's finally found what they've been looking for. That moment matters. That moment is sacred. And it only happens when you've done the work to show up consistently.

So, as you consider your next steps, ask yourself:

What platform feels natural to me?

Where can I show up consistently without resentment?

Which medium allows me to express my ideas most clearly?

What would it look like to go deep instead of wide?

When you answer those questions honestly, you'll find your lane. And once you've found it, trust it. Don't second-guess yourself just because someone else is getting more likes on Instagram. Likes don't build businesses. Trust does.

And that's what your core content channel is really about. It's about building a space—owned, consistent, and trustworthy—where your voice gets stronger, your message gets clearer, and your audience gets closer.

So keep showing up, whether you're writing articles, recording episodes, or filming videos. Build your camp in the desert, as we talked about earlier. Create an oasis your people can return to again and again. And as you do, remember that consistency is not a strategy. It's a form of love.

## Choosing Primary Platforms (and Letting the Rest Go)

One of the most freeing decisions you can make in your business is to stop trying to be everywhere. Everywhere sounds nice, in theory. The thought goes: the more places I show up, the more people will find me. But in reality, spreading yourself thin across every platform doesn't grow your business — it drains your energy and dilutes your message. It turns your brand into a scattered puzzle instead of a clear picture. That's why this section is so important: it's time to choose your primary platforms — and let the rest go.

There's a myth in the online space that to succeed, you must dominate every platform. Instagram, LinkedIn, Twitter, TikTok, YouTube, Pinterest, Medium — the list keeps growing. But the truth is, every platform has a culture. Every platform has its own language, its own algorithms, and its own expectations. Showing up meaningfully in just one of them takes time, thought, and care. Trying to show up in five? That's not a strategy — that's noise.

So, instead of being everywhere, focus on being fully present in the right places — the platforms where your audience already hangs out and where your natural style of communication can shine. This is where clarity meets efficiency.

Let's break it down.

**If you are in the B2B world or a coach or consultant who serves professionals,** your home should likely be LinkedIn. It's a space where decision-makers are actively looking for insight, growth, and solutions. It's not just a résumé database anymore — it's a hub for thought leadership. And the beauty of LinkedIn is that it rewards depth. You don't have to dance or perform or craft endless reels. You just have to show up consistently with real value.

**If your business is more lifestyle-driven, personal brand-based, or visually oriented,** then Instagram might be the best fit for you. Its platform thrives on aesthetics, storytelling, and daily glimpses into your world. It's the coffee shop of the internet — people go there to relax, scroll, and peek into the lives of others. But remember: don't mistake followers for connection. Use Instagram as a window, not a storefront. Let it lead people into a deeper experience with your brand — not be the whole experience.

Now, regardless of your industry, **email and podcasting** are two of the most stable, long-term platforms you can own. They're not subject to algorithm changes or shadow bans. They won't disappear overnight. And they allow you to speak directly into your audience's world — uninterrupted. Your email list is your digital Rolodex. It's how you stay in touch with your audience, no matter what happens on social media. Your podcast is your radio show — a consistent voice your audience can tune into on their terms.

So, how do you decide which ones to keep and which to let go?

Start by asking yourself three honest questions:

Where does my audience spend their time?

Where does my content style naturally fit?

Which platform can I show up on consistently — without resentment?

That third question might be the most important of all. Because here's the thing: you don't have to be on TikTok just because everyone else is. You don't have to blog if writing feels like pulling teeth. You don't have to make videos if you dread being on camera. There are a hundred ways to win — but not if you're forcing yourself to play someone else's game.

Pick your top one or two channels — your primary distribution platforms. These will become the vehicles for your message. Everything else? Let it go. Not forever, not out of fear — but because your time and energy are sacred. Focus is how you make progress. You don't build a brand by dipping your toes in every pool. You build it by swimming deep in one.

And once you've chosen, commit. Create a rhythm. Show up. Track your results. And most of all — let yourself go deep. Deep in your message. Deep in your connection. Deep in your service. Because that's where the transformation happens, that's where the trust builds. And that's what builds a real business.

Forget random acts of content. Forget chasing virality. Choose to build something that lasts.

## Don't Lose Sight of the Goal

At this stage in the journey, it's easy to become enamored with the machine you're building. You've learned how to identify your market, clarify your message, craft your value proposition, and build out a full distribution system. You're creating lead magnets, automating welcome sequences, and building long-term content ecosystems. You're starting to feel the momentum. The system is working. People are listening.

But before you go any further, I want to give you a gentle warning — and a powerful reminder: Don't lose sight of the goal.

It's possible — even tempting — to become a content machine. To fall in love with the process, the platforms, the numbers. You start checking open rates more than you check in with your audience. You focus on reach instead of relationships. You craft brilliant funnels but forget the human beings walking through them.

You see, content is a bridge — not a destination. The blog post, the podcast episode, the email — they're not the win. The win is the transformation you help create. The clarity you give someone who's been stuck. I hope you offer someone who's felt invisible. The freedom you spark in someone who finally sees a path forward.

That's the goal: **Connection. Trust. Transformation.** It's not about shouting louder. It's about whispering what matters — and being heard.

Owning your media is not about building a megaphone so you can broadcast to the world. It's about building a table where the right people can gather, listen, learn, and decide if they want to stay. And when you show up consistently, authentically, and with value, they stay. Not because you're flashy. Not because you have a million views. But because you became a trusted voice in a noisy world.

Remember, your audience doesn't need another guru. They need a guide. Someone who sees them. Someone who gets it. Someone who's previously walked the road and has the scars and wisdom to prove it.

So, as you wrap up this chapter and continue your journey of building, growing, and owning your media, take a breath. Take a moment. Reconnect with the heart behind all of this. The people you're serving. The problems you're solving. The impact you're creating.

You're not just building a content system. You're building a legacy.

Let's not forget why we started.

Let's not forget that behind every download is a person.

Behind every email address is a story.

Behind every subscription is a decision to trust you.

So write like it matters. Record like it's sacred. Serve like you remember what it felt like to be lost — and how much it meant to be found finally.

This is your moment. And the beautiful thing is —
you're doing it differently.

You're not building your house on rented land.
You're building something solid. Something sacred.
Something yours.

*Own your media. Own your message. Own your mission.*

And never, ever lose sight of the people you're doing
it for.

# Chapter 6: I – Implementing and Sustaining Your Media Platform

If you've made it this far into the journey, take a moment and appreciate something most entrepreneurs overlook: you didn't quit. That in itself sets you apart. Many people begin with passion. They get fired up at the start, excited by new possibilities, eager to escape social media noise, and finally own their voice. But along the way, the grind gets real. The idea of building something sustainable—not just shiny—feels heavy. And yet, here you are.

By now, you've carved out the essentials. You've defined your audience with clarity. You've discovered how to speak directly to them—not in slogans, but in words that matter. You've explored the various ways to show up consistently using the medium that suits you best: writing, speaking, or showing up on camera. Most importantly, you've started gently taking strangers and guiding them into your world—turning cold browsers into warm leads.

Now, it's time for the click.

This is the part where you shift from scattered effort to systematic execution. No more *"when I get time"* or *"maybe next week."* You're no longer guessing. You're building. This chapter is about moving from idea to infrastructure, from effort to ecosystem. It's where you take everything you've discovered about your market, message, and medium and lock it into a rhythm that grows with you.

Think of it like setting the foundation of a home you'll live in for years. The thrill of choosing paint colors and furniture is exciting, but without a strong foundation, none of that lasts. Implementation is the foundation. Sustainability is the framework. And your growth? That's what rises when the structure is solid.

But before you rush in and start pouring concrete and setting up walls, there's a necessary pause. A strategic breath. Here's the hard truth most content creators overlook: you can't scale what isn't working. You can't systematize what isn't aligned. You certainly shouldn't automate confusion, and that's why, before we talk about how to implement it, we begin with something far too many business owners skip—the audit.

## The Total Online Presence Audit: Your Strategic Starting Point

Imagine trying to renovate a house without checking if the foundation is cracked or the plumbing leaks behind the walls. That's what it's like to build a business without auditing your existing online presence. And that's why one of the most powerful tools we use at Livelong

Digital is the Total Online Presence Audit. This isn't a vanity report that tells you you've got a nice color scheme on your website or that your Instagram captions are witty. No, this is a comprehensive evaluation of your entire digital ecosystem—the stuff that makes or breaks your long-term success. It's designed to identify what's working, what's missing, and what's quietly sabotaging your growth.

Because let's be honest. Most business owners aren't running systems—they're performing random acts of marketing. One day, it's a post on Instagram. The next is an email blast sent to a list they haven't nurtured in months. Then comes a blog post written in a flurry of guilt because someone said, "You should blog more." There's no strategy. Just a series of good intentions duct-taped together with hope.

The Total Online Presence Audit puts a stop to that. It brings order to the chaos.

Here's how it works: the audit evaluates your website, your SEO performance, your content library, your social media channels, and—this is crucial—your lead capture and follow-up systems. It looks at the whole picture.

Not just how you look online but how you function. Not just whether you've posted lately but whether your message is aligned and your actions are consistent. Your website is the digital front door to your business. But is it welcoming? Is it clear who it's for and what it promises? Or is it an online brochure that leaves people confused? The audit examines your user journey—from the homepage to the contact form. It checks if your site is optimized for conversions, if your message is compelling, and if it's serving the audience you've worked so hard to define.

SEO is another area where business owners often underperform. And it's not their fault. SEO is complicated, technical, and often misunderstood. But here's the deal: over 90% of online experiences begin with a search. If you're not being found when people are searching for what you offer, you're invisible. The audit doesn't expect you to be an SEO wizard—it simply identifies what keywords you should be targeting, how your current content is performing, and what opportunities exist to get discovered more often by the right people.

Content strategy is next. This is about more than volume—it's about cohesion. Are your blog posts, podcasts, videos, and emails telling a unified story? Are they leading somewhere? Or are they fragmented pieces floating in the digital ether? The audit assesses whether your content builds momentum or bleeds energy. Because remember—your audience is on a journey. Your content is the map. If your map is incoherent, you'll lose them.

Then there's social media. We don't rely on it as the backbone of our business, but we can't ignore it either. The audit takes a hard look at your social presence. Are you using these platforms as distribution tools to lead people back to your owned media? Or are you just adding noise to an already loud room? We evaluate whether your social content is aligned with your brand message and if it's designed to spark engagement—not just likes but real conversations that build trust.

Finally, and most importantly, the audit investigates your lead capture and follow-up systems. This is where most businesses drop the ball. You might have great content and decent traffic—but if you're not turning those eyeballs into email subscribers and those subscribers into buyers, you're not building a business. You're building a hobby.

We assess your opt-in forms, lead magnets, welcome sequences, and conversion pathways. Are they clear? Are they compelling? Are they doing the job of moving people from curious to committed?

When all of this is complete, we hand you a roadmap. Not a one-size-fits-all plan. A personalized blueprint for building your media empire. We tell you exactly what's working and what needs improvement. We show you where your audience is getting stuck or slipping away. We also highlight the exact places where small changes could make a huge impact. But more than anything, the Total Online Presence Audit gives you peace of mind. It ensures you're not building a mansion on the sand. It anchors your future growth in a foundation of strategic clarity. Scan the QR Code to get your

**Total Online Presence Audit** ◼

Because here's the truth—content without strategy is noise. Marketing without alignment is a waste. And growth without infrastructure is chaos. That's why this audit is the starting line for every client we work with. And that's why we're putting it in your hands now.

So, if you've ever felt like you're spinning your wheels, creating content without traction, putting in effort without seeing returns—this is your moment to pause and reflect. To step back and take inventory. Not to criticize but to calibrate. Because you're not here to hustle aimlessly. You're here to build a legacy. And legacies don't get built by guessing.

In the next section, we'll dive into the actual mechanics of implementation—how to create a body of work that lives beyond a single post or campaign. But for now, this is your call to action: audit before you act. Step back before you sprint. Because once you see the whole picture clearly, you'll be able to build with confidence, intention, and direction.

And when that happens—when your foundation is secure, and your strategy is clear—everything else becomes easier. Marketing becomes intentional. Sales become natural. And growth becomes sustainable.

You've come this far. Let's build something that lasts.

Once you've completed your Total Online Presence Audit, what you hold in your hands is not just feedback—it's a mirror. It reflects the reality of how your digital footprint appears to those you're trying to serve. Now, it's time to begin building your body of work. Not randomly. Not impulsively. But intentionally. A successful media platform isn't built from sporadic blog posts or occasional social media updates—it's built from a well-organized foundation of value-rich content that works together as a system. This means creating a body of work: something that speaks even when you're sleeping, reaches new people while you're working, and continues to build your reputation without requiring your constant supervision.

Start by identifying your core themes. Think of them as the pillars that will support the house you're building. These big ideas define what you stand for and what your ideal audience comes to you to learn. A good rule of thumb is to choose three to five core topics. These themes shouldn't just be what you're passionate about but should also align with your audience's needs and wants. Your expertise matters, yes, but it must intersect with their curiosity, questions, and struggles. This is where the dance between your knowledge and their needs begins.

Now, once those core themes are identified, you can begin creating what's called "pillar content." This is your long-form, evergreen flagship content—timeless, in-depth, and foundational pieces. These are the blog posts, videos, or guides that a new visitor might find and think, "Wow, this is exactly what I've been looking for." Pillar content isn't trendy. It isn't reactive. It's the kind of content that serves today's reader and tomorrow's researcher. A detailed tutorial on your unique method. A case study showing your client's transformation. A guide to help your audience make a pivotal decision. These are all examples of pillar content that live on your website and form the spine of your brand.

But the journey doesn't end with pillar content. In fact, it's only the beginning. Once you've established these pillars, your next step is to use topic clustering to build around them. Think of it like creating a hub-and-spoke model: your core pillar sits in the center, and surrounding it are related pieces of content that reinforce, support, and drive traffic to it. This is the magic of topic clusters. For example, if your pillar content is a definitive guide on "The 5 Stages of Building a Digital Presence," your supporting content could include short blog posts on each stage, a podcast episode diving deeper into stage three, and an infographic summarizing the entire journey. Each piece links to the pillar, strengthening your authority in that space.

This clustering approach does more than just demonstrate expertise. It also boosts your discoverability through search engines. When Google sees multiple pieces of related content all pointing to a central hub, it reads that as an authority—and rewards you accordingly. But more importantly, it serves your reader. Because when they land on one piece, and it resonates, they'll naturally click to learn more. They stay in your world longer. They begin to trust your voice. They start to see you not just as another content creator but as a guide.

Once you've established your themes, created your pillar content, and built clusters around them, the next step is to stretch your efforts further through repurposing. This is where efficiency and creativity intersect. It's about making your content do more—work harder, live longer, reach farther. A blog post shouldn't just live as a blog post. It can become the script for a podcast episode. That podcast can be transcribed into a carousel post for LinkedIn. The carousel can become an infographic. That infographic can become part of a downloadable resource. Repurposing doesn't mean repeating yourself—it means respecting the effort you've already made by expanding its reach and meeting people where they are.

Think of your content like clay. Once it's formed into something substantial, it can be reshaped in many forms without losing its essence. This is especially useful when considering your audience's different learning styles and preferences. Some prefer to read. Others enjoy listening during their commute. Some like quick visuals. By repurposing, you're increasing accessibility without increasing your workload exponentially.

Now that you've begun to build this valuable body of work, it's time to make sure it doesn't just sit on your website collecting digital dust. That's where SEO comes in—not as a buzzword but as a strategy for sustainable visibility. With more than 90% of online journeys beginning with a search engine, you can't afford to ignore SEO. But let's demystify it. You can define SEO as *Simply Educating Others, or perhaps Simply Entertaining Others.* SEO isn't about gaming the system or stuffing your posts with keywords. It's about creating content that aligns with what your audience is already searching for—and organizing it in a way that search engines can understand.

Start by conducting keyword research. But don't just look for the most popular terms. Instead, focus on specific questions your audience is asking. These long-tail keywords are often less competitive, more specific, and more valuable. A generic keyword like "online marketing" might be hard to rank for, but "how to create a nurture sequence for a coaching business" is far more targeted—and if someone's searching for it, they're probably exactly your kind of person.

When you write your content, weave those keywords in naturally. Use them in your titles, your subheadings, and your meta descriptions. Make sure your images have descriptive alt text. Link between your pieces of content strategically. These little adjustments might seem technical, but they're acts of service—because they help the right people find your work at the exact moment they need it.

And when they find it, what should they see? Clear calls to action. Every piece of content you create should offer a next step. A lead magnet to download. A checklist to complete. An invitation to book a discovery call. This is how content becomes a funnel—not in the pushy, manipulative way we sometimes imagine, but as a series of helpful nudges. "Here's something useful. Want more? Here's how to get it." That's what turns strangers into subscribers and subscribers into clients.

But let's take it even further. Once someone opts in and raises their hand and says, "Yes, I'm interested", what happens next? This is where email marketing comes into play. A solid SEO strategy brings people in. A strong email sequence keeps them engaged. This is the nurturing part of your funnel. It's where you continue the conversation, build rapport, and earn trust—not through gimmicks, but through value.

Use your emails to send them the kind of content they can't wait to read. Answer their questions. Share behind-the-scenes stories. Show them the real person behind the brand. Make them feel seen. That's how you guide people from curious browsers to committed buyers.

And when the time is right—when you've delivered value, demonstrated your expertise, and connected on a human level—then you make the offer. That's the final step in the funnel: conversion. But here's the key: the sale isn't the end of the relationship. It's the beginning. When someone buys from you, they're saying, "I trust you to take me to my next level." Honor that trust by continuing to deliver, serve, and guide.

So, to summarize where we are, you're now not just creating content. You're creating an ecosystem. A living, breathing system that brings people into your world, walks with them through their transformation, and ultimately allows you to grow your business sustainably and joyfully. No more guessing. No more random acts of marketing. Just strategic, soul-aligned action. That's the beauty of owning your media. And that's the power of building a body of work that will serve your business and your audience for years.

## Your Signature Framework Starts With You

If you've followed everything up to this point, then by now, you've built a strong foundation. You've done the hard internal work — identifying your market, shaping your message, choosing your media modality, and developing distribution systems that convert casual onlookers into curious prospects. And now, the time has come to define something deeply powerful, something only you can truly own: your Intellectual Property, not in the legal sense, but in the form of a recognizable, memorable, and transformational process that reflects your essence and positions you as the go-to expert in your space.

This is where we talk about your **signature method**.

You might be thinking, "What do I have that others don't?" And the answer is simple: your story, your experiences, your process. You've lived a unique life. You've developed skills, tools, and insights that others are still searching for. But too many people bury those gifts under the assumption that it's "nothing special." That ends today. Because the truth is, the path you've walked — with all its missteps, pivots, and hard-won lessons — is the roadmap your clients hope to find. They don't want abstract theories; they want something human. They want something real. They want something repeatable. And what better way to give them that than through a method that bears your name?

Start with your name. Write it down in all capital letters. Then, insert a dot between each letter, like this: J.O.H.N.S.O.N. Each letter becomes a step of your process. Each step represents a piece of your philosophy, a stage in your client's transformation, or a core value you stand for. For instance:

J — Justify your goals

O — Organize your efforts

H — Harness your skills

N — Navigate obstacles

S — Strategize for growth

O — Optimize for Impact

N — Nurture long-term results

Do you see what just happened there? Out of seven letters, you've built a seven-step framework. That, right there, is a signature method. And even if your name is shorter or longer, the same principle applies. Whether you have four letters or ten, the acronym you create will become your framework — the blueprint that guides your clients through the results they crave.

The beauty of this model lies not just in its memorability but in its authenticity. It's rooted in you — your insights, your voice, your process. No one can duplicate it because it comes from a place no algorithm or copycat can replicate: your lived experience. That's why this step matters. It's your stake in the ground, the flag that says, "This is who I am, and this is how I help."

Now, your new framework isn't just a clever acronym. It becomes the narrative spine of your brand. It gives structure to your keynote speeches. It gives life to your book chapters. It informs the format of your podcast episodes, your workshops, and your courses. And perhaps most importantly, it anchors your marketing in something solid, something that isn't borrowed or built on trends but something that reflects your truth.

People don't just buy products — they buy processes. They want certainty. They want to follow a roadmap that's been proven to work. And when that roadmap has your name on it, they begin to associate their progress with your brand. That's how trust is built. That's how reputations are formed. That's how you become unforgettable.

## From Framework to Offers: Building Your Product Ladder

Once your method is defined, the next step is to shape it into layers of value. This is where we talk about productizing your method. Think of your framework as a recipe. Depending on how your audience wants to engage, you can offer a taste, a meal, or the whole seven-course experience. Regardless of size, each offering pulls from the same central idea: your unique method.

Let's break it down into a practical structure — what we call the Product Ladder. Imagine four levels, each ascending in depth, duration, and price. These levels give people multiple ways to work with you, depending on their needs, their budget, and their readiness. And they all use the same methodology — meaning you're not reinventing the wheel every time you create something new.

Level one could be a 7-hour live or virtual workshop. This is the most accessible format — a concentrated immersion into your method. It's fast, impactful, and perfect for those seeking quick wins. You can walk them through each step, provide exercises, and give them a practical sense of your approach. This could be a high-value, low-barrier introduction to your ecosystem, priced at $375.

From there, you might offer a 7-day challenge. This is more experiential. Here, you walk your audience through each step over the course of a week, guiding them with daily tasks, check-ins, or group accountability. It's an opportunity for transformation and community. It offers deeper engagement and is often delivered through a combination of email prompts, videos, or live group sessions. This kind of experience might be priced at $999, and it becomes a powerful bridge between interest and real investment.

Level three is the 7-week coaching program. This is for those ready to commit to long-term change. Each week is devoted to a step in your process, with time for integration, support, and reflection. This is where real transformation happens — not just because of your method but because of your presence. Clients see you as their guide. You are no longer a vendor; you are a mentor. Pricing for this level could range between $1450 to $2000, depending on how you deliver it (group vs. one-on-one).

And finally, at the top of the ladder is your 7-month mentorship. This is for clients who want the full experience — the deep dive. Here, you're not just walking them through your method. You're building something together. This might include private coaching, in-depth implementation support, personalized audits, or even in-person retreats. This is your premium offer. And because it's anchored in the same methodology as every other product, it doesn't feel like a leap — it feels like a logical progression. You've simply increased the depth, access, and value.

The power of this product ladder isn't just in its structure — it's in its simplicity. You're using one method, one system, and simply repackaging it to meet your audience where they are. You're reducing overwhelm for yourself while increasing options for your audience. This is what makes your business sustainable. You're no longer scrambling to create something new every time someone expresses interest. Instead, you're pointing them to the right step on the ladder. They ascend at their own pace, but every step deepens their relationship with your brand.

And here's another benefit: having this kind of system eliminates one of the biggest bottlenecks in online business — inconsistent delivery. Because when you productize your method, your process becomes predictable. Your client experience becomes repeatable. And your outcomes become scalable. Whether you're delivering to ten people or a hundred, your framework holds steady. You're no longer trading time for money — you're trading transformation for trust.

If you're worried, this means you'll run out of things to say. Think again. Once you have a method, it becomes a content goldmine. Each step in your framework can become a blog post, a podcast topic, a chapter in your book, or even a story in your newsletter. You're no longer staring at a blank page; you're building out the pillars of your thought leadership. You've got structure. You've got focus. And now, you've got momentum.

This is where your method begins to breathe. This is where it becomes more than a clever acronym — it becomes a living, breathing ecosystem. Each time you share your method — whether through teaching, speaking, writing, or podcasting — you're reinforcing your authority. You're embedding yourself in the minds of your audience. You're giving them language to describe the problem they're facing and the solution you offer. That kind of clarity is rare. And that kind of resonance is what sets you apart.

It's worth repeating here: people do business with those they know, like, and trust. But trust doesn't come from shouting the loudest or showing up the most often. Trust comes from consistency. From clarity. From confidence. And nothing builds all three quite like a signature method. Once you have it, it becomes your anchor. Your filter. Your foundation. Every decision — from content creation to product development — gets easier because it's tethered to something true.

So take a breath, and take this seriously. Your IP is your legacy. It's the proof of your path, the systematization of your soul's work. And it's the most powerful tool you'll ever own — because no one else can ever take it from you. Let this be the chapter where it all starts to make sense. The noise fades. The distractions fall away. And what's left is you — your method, your voice, your impact.

You don't need to do more. You need to own what you already have.

And that's where everything changes.

## Lead Magnet + Funnel Implementation

By now, you've likely realized that success in this journey isn't about flashy ads or slick slogans—it's about creating real connections and consistent value. At the heart of that connection lies a simple yet powerful concept: your lead magnet. A lead magnet is an entry point. It's your handshake. Your introduction. It's a small, digestible piece of value that solves a very specific problem your audience is already facing. But here's the secret—it shouldn't solve everything. It should solve just enough to earn their attention, prove you understand their world, and leave them wanting more.

Think of it like offering someone a sip of the best coffee they've ever had. They might not be ready to buy the whole bag of beans or sign up for a subscription, but now they know where the good stuff comes from—and they're not going to forget it. Good lead magnets are easy to consume, actionable, and instantly useful. They don't overwhelm. Instead, they whisper: "Hey, I understand what you're going through. Let me make your day a little easier." That's all it takes to open the door to deeper trust.

You don't have to overcomplicate it either. Quizzes, one-page blueprints, sample audio lessons, simple checklists, and micro eBooks work beautifully. For instance, if you're a coach, a "5-Minute Clarity Quiz" can help a visitor discover what's holding them back. If you're in wellness, a one-page "Energy Reset Guide" might be just the thing. What matters is that it's relevant, quick to absorb, and positioned as the first step toward a larger transformation.

Once someone opts in for your lead magnet, your funnel begins. Don't let that word intimidate you. A funnel is simply a journey you've designed for someone after they say "yes" to you. It typically starts with an opt-in page, where the lead magnet lives. Keep this page clear and focused. Use headlines that speak directly to their pain point and a short form that asks for nothing more than their name and email. Don't ask for a phone number unless it's essential. Simplicity wins.

After the opt-in comes the email sequence. This is where you turn strangers into warm prospects, gently guiding them through a conversation with you—just like we've been doing in this book. A three-part email sequence works wonderfully:

**Email 1: Know You** — Introduce yourself. Tell your story. Share the "why" behind your work. This is about being relatable, not impressive. You're just letting them know they're in the right place.

**Email 2: Like You** — Give them something valuable. This could be an insight, a behind-the-scenes look, a tip, or even a personal moment that connects emotionally. You're building rapport, proving your expertise, and helping without pushing.

**Email 3: Trust You** — This is where you can include social proof, a short case study, or a testimonial. It's your opportunity to invite them to take the next step.

Maybe it's a discovery call, a mini-course, or a low-ticket product that allows them to experience your value at a deeper level.

That's it. Simple, respectful, and human. Show them you can help by actually helping them. That's the only funnel you'll ever need to begin with. No pressure tactics. No countdown timers. No spammy sales language. Just consistent, thoughtful service.

This system—lead magnet, email sequence, conversion point—is the backbone of turning attention into action. And because you've already clarified your audience and created a strong value proposition, this part becomes a natural extension. It's not marketing in the old sense of the word. It's just relationship-building at scale.

You don't need thousands of followers to make this work. You just need a few dozen right people coming through a well-thought-out funnel every month. With time and consistency, that's all it takes to build something truly remarkable.

## Alternative Marketing Channels (Beyond Social Media)

If there's one thing we've repeated throughout this book, it's this: you don't need to depend on social media to grow your business. There are countless paths to visibility and trust that don't require playing games with algorithms, dancing for views, or scrolling endlessly just to stay "relevant." The digital landscape is vast. And if you can commit to owning your message and serving with clarity, you can thrive on your own terms.

Let's look at some proven strategies operating outside the typical social media loop. These approaches give you leverage, authority, and reach—all without feeding the beast.

**YouTube Funnels** are an excellent way to offer deep, searchable content. A well-planned series of short, specific videos can walk someone from cold awareness into warm engagement without ever needing to post a single story or reel. Each video becomes a trust-building asset that works 24/7.

**Podcasting** lets you speak directly to the hearts and minds of your audience. Podcasts are intimate, consistent, and powerful for long-form storytelling. And when you bring guests on board, you also gain access to their audiences. It's a relationship amplifier.

**Guest Blogging** gives you access to audiences you don't have to build from scratch. When you write a high-value article for an existing platform in your niche, you borrow their trust and visibility. Do this a few times, and you'll be seen as an expert in your field.

**Guest Speaking** and **Conference Panels** open up powerful in-person and virtual networking opportunities. Whether it's a local business group, a professional association, or an online summit, getting in front of a live audience positions you as an authority—no likes or followers required.

**Teaching Workshops** or short courses help you anchor your expertise in people's minds. When you teach, you lead. People remember teachers. They trust them. And they come back when they're ready to go deeper.

**Public Relations (PR)** is one of the most underused tools in digital entrepreneurship. Getting featured in a local paper, a niche podcast, or an industry magazine isn't just about ego. It's about credibility. You're borrowing the authority of others and reinforcing your message to new audiences.

**Affiliate Programs** create win-win scenarios. You allow others to promote your product or service and reward them for it. This expands your reach while building a community around your offer.

**Direct Mail** might feel old school, but it still works. A well-designed postcard, handwritten note, or physical sample can leave a lasting impression—especially in a digital world where almost no one does it.

**Answering Questions on Platforms Like Quora** allows you to demonstrate expertise and link back to your site or resources. It's subtle, organic, and long-tail—perfect for playing the long game.

**Medium, Substack, and Other Writing Platforms** allow you to syndicate your content and build visibility without being chained to algorithms. Your work lives on, searchable, sharable, and often discoverable months or years after you publish it.

Other options include **nonprofit partnerships, sponsoring events, publishing in industry-specific journals**, and more. The point is this: visibility doesn't start or end with Instagram, Facebook, or TikTok. In fact, those platforms often give you the *illusion* of connection while offering very little control.

So here's what I want you to do. Choose two or three of these channels that align with your strengths and values. Don't try to do everything. Just pick what feels sustainable and enjoyable. If you love speaking, lean into podcasting and guest speaking. If you enjoy writing, explore Medium, newsletters, and guest blogging. If you're more visual, consider YouTube or even hosting a free workshop.

Remember, the goal here isn't volume—it's consistency. The Internet is flooded with noise. You don't need to shout louder. You need to show up steadily and say something that matters.

You've already done the heavy lifting. You've clarified your message. You've identified your audience. You've started building your platform. These marketing channels are simply the next logical step. They help you distribute your story in places where people are already listening.

And the best part? You're not dependent. You're not a renter. You're the owner of your ideas, messages, systems, and results. These alternative paths are not backup plans—they are the future for those who want to build a real business that lasts.

## Sustaining the System: How to Keep Going Without Burning Out

At this point, you've done what most never will. You've crafted your message, chosen your medium, implemented a funnel, and started to transform scattered visibility into strategic connection. But now comes the most underestimated part of all — staying in the game.

If creating your media platform was like planting seeds, sustaining it is the daily watering, weeding, and nurturing that turns it into a thriving garden. And just like any garden, it doesn't bloom overnight. This is where patience and persistence take center stage. The loudest voices online aren't always the best — often, they're just the ones who've stuck around long enough to be heard. It's not about going viral. It's about being visible consistently.

One of the biggest misconceptions people have about owning their media is that it will instantly explode with traffic, leads, and income. They forget that relationships take time. Earning trust — real trust — takes time. The people who find you through your emails, podcasts, blogs, or newsletters might not be ready to hire you today. Some may not be ready for a year. But if your content consistently speaks to their needs, they'll remember you when they are. And when they're ready, they won't search for a "marketing expert" or "life coach." They'll search for you by name. This is why having a realistic weekly routine is essential. The goal isn't to churn content like a machine but to show up consistently — even if that means showing up once a week with intention. Your weekly content plan should be grounded in three core activities: create, repurpose, and distribute. Maybe every Monday, you write or record a piece of content — a podcast, a blog, a solo video. Then, Tuesday is your repurposing day. That content becomes an email, a LinkedIn post, maybe a reel. Wednesday through Friday is distribution and engagement: sharing your message across chosen platforms, replying to emails, commenting on responses, and connecting deeper with your community.

You don't need to be everywhere. You don't need to do everything. You just need to do the right things consistently. And the right things are the ones that help your audience move closer to their goals. This is how you become their guide — not their savior, guru, or consistent, reliable guide.

As you move forward, your job is to monitor what's working and what's not. Data will help you course correct. Which emails get opened? Which podcast episodes spark replies? Which blog posts drive traffic? Don't become obsessed with metrics, but do pay attention to patterns. What's resonating? Where is your audience clicking, pausing, commenting, replying? These are your cues.

Most importantly, never stop learning. Update your voice. Refresh your knowledge. Stay curious. If you're serving coaches, consultants, business owners — even individuals seeking transformation — your relevance depends on your evolution. You're not just building a brand. You're building a reputation, and reputation grows when the content behind it continues to get sharper, clearer, and more valuable over time.

And don't do it alone. Invite your audience into the process. Ask them what they want more of. Let them co-create the content with you through their feedback, questions, and responses. This builds something more valuable than attention — it builds belonging.

If you ever feel tired, remember this: you're not running on a treadmill; you're building a library, a vault of value that compounds with time. Every piece of content you create is a digital asset. It works while you sleep. It's searchable, referable, and scalable. Unlike a social media post that disappears after 24 hours, your podcast episodes, blog posts, and newsletters live on. They become your voice in rooms you haven't entered yet.

Your system doesn't need to be complex to be sustainable. It needs to be real, repeatable, and rooted in your great work. That's how you stay in the game without burning out. That's how you build a brand that lasts.

## Building a Legacy Through Media Ownership

At some point, this journey shifts. What started as marketing becomes meaning. What started as content creation becomes an influence. And what started as a business strategy becomes a legacy.

When you own your media, you don't just build awareness — you build authority. You stop depending on platforms to validate you. You stop worrying about whether the algorithm smiled at you today. You start showing up because you have something to say — and people who trust you to say it.

Your media platform becomes the most valuable asset in your business. It's not your logo. It's not even your offer. It's your voice, story, perspective, and process — consistently expressed and accessible to those you're here to serve. This is what clients remember. This is what they share. This is what keeps your business alive in someone's mind until the moment they need you.

Think about your favorite author, coach, or teacher. Chances are, they didn't just post occasionally on Facebook. They had a body of work. They had a message. They had a system and shared it consistently in their own space. That's what you're doing now.

This is about more than marketing. It's about transformation. When someone finds your podcast at 2 a.m. because they're worried about their business, and your voice calms their nerves — that's legacy. When a reader prints out your blog post and tapes it to their desk — that's legacy. When someone hears your framework and suddenly understands how to move forward — that's legacy.

You don't have to be famous to make an impact. You just have to be findable. And when you own your media, you're findable in all the right ways. Your message isn't buried under trending hashtags. It's not lost in a sea of scrollable noise. It's searchable, savable, and shareable. And over time, it becomes synonymous with the result you deliver.

Legacy is built in the ordinary moments. It's in the weekly podcast episode you almost skipped. It's in the email you wrote when you didn't feel inspired but still showed up. It's in the consistent decision to keep going — to keep showing up — even when the return isn't immediate.

And one day, that consistency compounds. Your inbox is full. Your calendar is booked. Your name gets mentioned in rooms you've never entered. People quote your frameworks. They teach your methods. They become advocates of your brand not because you shouted the loudest but because you whispered the clearest, the most consistently.

That's the power of owning your media. You shape your narrative. You steer your story. And over time, your presence becomes a place people return to — not because they have to, but because they want to.

Let that sink in. You're not just building a business. You're building a home for your ideas. A home for transformation. A home for every person who's been searching for someone who truly gets it.

So keep going. The next email, podcast, and message might just be the one that changes everything — for them and for you.

## Create Your Unique Method Today

You've come a long way, and now it's time to forge something distinctly yours — something no one else can replicate. At this point in your journey, it's no longer just about strategy or execution. It's about identity. And the most powerful identity you can create in business is the one tied to your own name — your unique method.

Let's begin with something incredibly simple. Write your name in capital letters. Just your first name is enough for now. Then, place a dot between each letter. That's your framework. Each letter becomes a guiding point — a stepping stone for someone else's transformation.

This exercise isn't about vanity. It's about clarity. When you build your signature methodology using your name, you give your audience something they can remember, repeat, and rely on. Think of it as your business's DNA — embedded with your values, experience, and approach. You're not borrowing someone else's roadmap. You're carving out your own.

Take the letter J, for example. It might stand for "Justify your goal" — the first step in helping your audience commit to change. O might be "Organize your thoughts," H could become "Harness your skills," and so on. The beauty is in the customization. Each step represents a tactical move and an emotional layer of the journey your clients will go through.

The next step is to flesh out your acronym with clear, benefit-driven language. Don't worry about jargon or sounding like an industry expert — focus instead on how your audience speaks, how they feel, and what they fear. They're not looking for brilliance; they're looking for resonance. They want to feel understood. Your acronym should speak their language, not yours.

Once you have your framework, turn it into a roadmap. Each step becomes a piece of content — a podcast episode, a blog, a live video, a workshop, or an email sequence. Suddenly, you're not staring at a blank screen. You're not scrambling for topics. You're following a path — one you created — and your audience is right there with you, step by step.

This is what it means to build a legacy. Not only are you solving problems and showing up consistently, but you're anchoring your presence in something uniquely recognizable. Your framework is your voice. It's your fingerprint on your industry. And the best part? No one else can claim it because no one else is you.

Now, pause for a moment. Look at what you've built. You've taken what felt like noise — scattered ideas, half-built funnels, mixed messages — and turned it into a symphony. Each note is composed by you. This isn't just implementation. This is ownership.

You are now the architect of a system that allows you to create without burnout, teach without confusion, and serve without dilution. People will know you by this method. They'll refer to it, share it, and ask about it. You've created your own intellectual property — and in doing so, you've crafted your own category. You're no longer competing. You're leading.

Your method, your IP, will be the backbone of every offer, every course, every keynote speech, and every discovery call. And because it's so deeply rooted in your truth, it will be sustainable. It won't feel forced. It won't require performance. It will flow.

Now imagine how you'll feel when someone introduces you as "the creator of the [Y.O.U.R. N.A.M.E] Method." That's not just branding. That's authority. And you earned it by showing up, doing the work, and codifying your story into a framework the world can follow.

So go ahead. Turn your name into a movement. Let every letter represent a promise to your audience. Then, deliver on those promises through every piece of content, every client interaction, and every lesson you teach.

Ownership looks like this — not in theory, but in practice.

There's a moment in every journey where the fog begins to lift. The road is still long, but the direction is clear. That's where you are now. And I want to take a moment to say — you've done something powerful. Most people won't make it this far. They'll stay stuck in the loop of trying, tweaking, abandoning, and repeating. But you? You've chosen clarity over chaos.

Yes, it's a lot. Yes, it can feel overwhelming. But I want you to know that every great business is built on one page, one post, and one podcast at a time. Don't try to do it all. Just do what matters most — today. Then, show up again tomorrow. Consistency compounds faster than intensity.

What the world needs right now isn't more content. It's more connection. More leaders are willing to speak with heart, serve with conviction, and build with integrity. The world doesn't need another viral video or a perfectly branded funnel. It needs you. Your story. Your way. Your method. Your voice. So if you're sitting here thinking, "Where do I start?" — go back to your notes. Pick one action step. Just one. Maybe it's writing your name and turning it into an acronym. Maybe it's recording your first podcast. Maybe it's finally publishing that blog post that's been sitting in drafts for weeks. Whatever it is, move toward it.

And as you do, remember this: owning your media isn't about vanity. It's about visibility. It's not about ego. It's about empathy. It's not about being louder. It's about being clearer. Owning your media means you no longer wait for permission. You write your own rules. You build your own platform. You tell your story your way — and invite the right people to come along for the journey.

You've worked hard to reach this point. You've identified your market, refined your message, selected your media, and built the early bones of your system. Now, you're not just someone with a business idea. You're a creator with a mission. A guide with a map. A leader with a legacy in the making.

And legacies aren't built overnight. They're built in quiet hours, with thoughtful action and unwavering belief. They're built by those who choose structure over noise, clarity over chaos, and truth over trends.

So go ahead. *Own your media. Own your message. Own your mission.*

And if no one has told you lately, I'm proud of you.

Let's build what only you can build.

Promise?

# Chapter 7: Putting It All Together

First, let me say something important: you made it this far. That puts you ahead of 95% of people who start reading business books or take courses. Most people get excited in the beginning, read a few chapters, maybe take some notes, and then... life happens. The book gets buried under a pile of mail, the course login gets forgotten, and six months later, they're buying another book, hoping this one will be different.

But you're still here. You've stuck with it through seven chapters of market research, message development, lead generation strategies, and all the foundational work that most people want to skip. You've done the hard part that isn't sexy or exciting but is absolutely necessary.

You've learned how to define your market, so you know exactly who you're talking to. You've crafted your message so it actually connects with real people who have real problems. You've figured out your medium — whether that's podcasting, writing, video, or speaking — and you understand how to generate leads consistently instead of hoping and praying that someone will magically find you.

That's huge. That's the foundation that 90% of struggling business owners never build properly. They jump straight to trying to sell stuff without doing any of this groundwork, and then they wonder why nobody's buying. But here's what I've learned after working with thousands of entrepreneurs: having the knowledge isn't enough. Information without implementation is just expensive entertainment. You can know everything about building a business and still be broke if you never actually do anything with what you know.

This chapter is different. This is where we shift from learning to doing. This is where you transform from someone who knows how to build a business to someone who actually has one. This is your implementation blueprint.

Here's the thing I want you to burn into your brain: *You don't need more information. You need more implementation.*

I see this all the time. People come to me and say, "I need to learn more about email marketing," "I need to understand funnels better," or "I should probably read another book about sales." And when I ask them what they've actually implemented from what they already know, there's this long pause.

They know enough to get started. They know enough to make money. But they keep consuming instead of creating because consuming feels productive without being risky. Learning feels like progress without the possibility of failure.

But here's the truth: you're going to fail sometimes. That's not a bug in the system. It's a feature. Every failure teaches you something that no book or course ever could. Every mistake gets you closer to what actually works for your specific situation with your specific audience.

So, if you take nothing else from this chapter, take this: stop collecting information and start creating and implementing. The world doesn't need another person who knows how to build a business. The world needs you to actually build yours.

## Reality Check: Stepping Off the Platform

Let me tell you about one of the scariest moments in building an online business. It's the moment you decide to step off the platform.

What do I mean by that? I mean the moment you stop relying on other people's audiences and start building your own. The moment you transition from borrowed attention to owned attention. The moment you go from being a tenant to being a landlord in the digital real estate game.

Up until now, maybe you've been posting on social media and getting likes and comments. Maybe you've been guesting on other people's podcasts or writing for other people's blogs. Maybe you've been speaking at events or networking at meetups. All of that stuff is great, and it's an important part of getting started.

But there comes a point where you have to step off the platform and start building your own world.

And when you do that, it gets quiet. Really quiet.

When you're posting on Facebook, you get immediate feedback. People like your stuff; they comment and share. You feel connected. You feel like you're making progress. There's this constant stream of little dopamine hits that tell you you're doing something right.

But when you start your own podcast, launch your own newsletter, or build your own website... crickets, at least at first.

You put out your first podcast episode, and two people download it. One of them is your mom. You send your first newsletter to your list of twelve subscribers, but nobody replies. You write a blog post that takes you four hours, and it gets zero comments.

This is where most people quit.

They think something's wrong. They think they made a mistake. They think maybe they should go back to posting on Instagram because at least people were engaging there. But here's what's really happening: you're building something real instead of something borrowed.

You're creating an asset instead of just creating content for someone else's asset. When you post on social media, you're basically working for free on Facebook, Instagram, or LinkedIn. You're creating content that makes their platform more valuable, and in exchange, they give you a little bit of reach. But that reach can disappear overnight if they change their algorithm, if your account gets suspended, or if they just decide they don't like you anymore.

When you build your own platform – your own podcast, your own email list, your own website – nobody can take that away from you. You own the relationship with your audience. You control how you communicate with them. You decide what messages they see and when they see them.

But it requires a different mindset. Instead of optimizing for immediate feedback, you're optimizing for long-term asset building. Instead of chasing likes and shares, you're building deep relationships with people who actually care about what you have to say.

I'm not saying you should abandon social media completely. But I am saying you should think of it as a way to drive people to your own platform, not as your main platform.

The loneliness and doubt you feel when you make this transition is normal. It's part of the process. You're not doing anything wrong. You're just building something that will last instead of something that feels good right now. Every successful business owner I know has gone through this phase. They all remember the early days when they were talking to what felt like an empty room. But they kept going because they understood that building something real takes time.

Think of it like moving from a crowded apartment building to your own house. In the apartment building, there's always noise and activity and people around. When you move to your own house, especially if it's in a new neighborhood, it's quiet. You might feel isolated at first. But now you have space to grow. You have control over your environment. You can build exactly what you want without having to follow someone else's rules.

That's what stepping off the platform feels like. It's scary at first, but it's the only way to build something that's truly yours.

## Real Case Study: From Facebook Ban to Full Podcast Empire

Let me remind you of my story that changed everything for me and taught me the most important lesson about building an independent business.

A few years ago, I was doing pretty well on Facebook. I had built up a decent following, was getting good engagement on my posts, and was actually making money from the connections I was making on the platform. I felt like I had figured out the social media game. Then, one morning, I woke up to find my Facebook account had been suspended. No warning. No explanation. Just gone.

At first, I thought it was a mistake. I reached out to Facebook support, filled out their forms, and waited for a response. Days went by. Then weeks. I tried creating new accounts, but they would get suspended within hours. Apparently, I was permanently banned from the platform.

To this day, I have no idea what I did wrong. Maybe it was something I posted. Maybe someone reported me. Maybe their algorithm just didn't like me. It doesn't matter. What matters is that overnight, my entire business presence disappeared.

I felt sick. Not just because I lost my following but because I realized how vulnerable I had made myself. I had built my entire business on someone else's platform, and they took it away without explanation or recourse.

But here's the thing about getting punched in the face by life: it clarifies things real quickly.

I had always known I should start a podcast. I had been thinking about it for months, maybe even years. But there was always a reason to wait. I needed better equipment. I needed to plan out more episodes. I needed to figure out the perfect format. I needed to wait until I had more time.

But when Facebook disappeared, I didn't have the luxury of waiting anymore. I had to do something, and I had to do it fast.

So I started a podcast called *The Online Prosperity Experience*. It's not a perfect podcast. Not a well-planned podcast. Just a podcast.

I used the microphone on my laptop. I recorded episodes in my kitchen. I didn't have fancy intro music or professional editing. I just talked about the stuff I knew and cared about.

The first few episodes were rough. I stumbled over words. I had long pauses while I figured out what to say next. I said "um" and "uh" way too much. But I published them anyway.

And here's what I discovered: people didn't care that it wasn't perfect. They cared that it was helpful.

The downloads started slow – maybe 20 or 30 people per episode. But then something interesting happened. People started leaving comments. Not just "great episode" comments, but real comments. People sharing their own stories. People are asking follow-up questions.

People told me how what I shared helped them with their specific situation.

This was different from social media engagement. These weren't quick likes or emoji reactions. These were thoughtful responses from people who had spent 20 or 30 minutes listening to what I had to say. The quality of engagement was completely different. More importantly, these people were finding me because they were looking for solutions to problems, not because they were mindlessly scrolling through a feed. They had searched for podcasts about my topic. They had intentionally chosen to download and listen to my show. They were self-selecting as people who cared about what I had to offer.

The emotional turbulence of that transition was intense. Some days, I felt like I was making progress. Other days, I felt like I was talking to nobody. There were times I wanted to give up and go back to trying to rebuild on social media. But I kept getting these comments that reminded me why I was doing this. Someone would write a paragraph about how a specific episode helped them solve a problem they'd been struggling with for months. Someone else would ask a question that led to a great idea for a new episode. Someone would share their own experience that taught me something new.

That's when I realized something crucial: the message matters more than the messenger. People weren't following me on Facebook because they loved me personally. They were following me because I was sharing information that helped them. And those people didn't disappear when Facebook banned me. They were still out there, still looking for solutions to their problems. The podcast became proof that the market for my message existed outside of any specific platform. If people were willing to seek out my content, download it, listen to it, and engage with it, that meant there was real demand for what I had to offer.

Six months after starting the podcast, I was getting more meaningful engagement than I ever had on Facebook. A year later, I had turned that podcast into multiple revenue streams. Two years later, I had built a business that was completely independent of any social media platform. Getting banned from Facebook was the best thing that ever happened to my business. It forced me to build something real instead of something borrowed. It taught me that platforms come and go, but valuable content and genuine relationships last forever.

But more than that, it taught me that you don't need permission to build a business. You don't need a big platform, a huge following, or perfect equipment. You just need something valuable to say and the willingness to say it consistently.

The podcast comments became my new feedback loop. Instead of likes and shares, I was having real conversations with real people who had real problems I could solve. That feedback helped me understand my audience better, refine my message, and eventually create offers that people actually wanted to buy.

## Building the Feedback Loop

Here's something most people get wrong about building an audience: they think passive consumption is enough. They think if people are listening to their podcasts, reading their blog, or watching their videos, that's success.

But passive consumption doesn't build a business. Active engagement does.

The goal isn't just to have people consume your content. The goal is to turn those passive listeners into active participants in your world. You want to move them from being consumers to being community members.

This is where most content creators leave money on the table. They create great content, people consume it, and then... nothing. The audience member goes back to their life, and the creator hopes they'll remember to check out the next piece of content.

But what if you could capture that moment when someone is most engaged with your content and turn it into an ongoing relationship?

That's exactly what a proper feedback loop does.

Here's how it works: During your podcast (or in your blog post or video), you mention a specific resource that complements what you're talking about. Maybe it's a checklist, a template, a guide, or a tool. Something that takes the ideas you just shared and makes them immediately actionable. But here's the key: they can't just download it. They have to give you their email address to get it.

This isn't about being sneaky or trying to trick people. This is about creating a fair exchange of value. You're giving them something useful that took you time and effort to create. In exchange, they're giving you permission to continue the conversation.

Let me give you a specific example. Let's say you just recorded a podcast episode about email marketing for small businesses. During the episode, you walk through the five types of emails every business should send to new subscribers. At the end of the episode, you say something like:

"If you want to see exactly what these five emails look like, I've put together a complete template pack that shows you word-for-word examples of each email, plus the subject lines I use and the timing for when to send them. You can grab that free template pack at yourwebsite.com/emailtemplates."

When people go to that page, they enter their email address and get immediate access to the templates. But now you have their contact information, which means you can continue the conversation beyond just that one episode.

This is where the magic happens. That person went from being a passive listener to being an active participant. They raised their hand and said, "Yes, I want more of this." They've given you permission to email them with related content, ideas, and offers.

And here's what's beautiful about this system: the people who take this step are self-selecting as your best prospects. They're not just casual listeners who happened to stumble across your content. They're people who are actively looking for solutions to problems you can solve.

Your email list becomes a collection of people who have already demonstrated interest in what you offer. When you email them, you're not interrupting them with random marketing messages. You're continuing a conversation they opted into.

But it gets better. Now you can survey these people. You can ask them what their biggest challenges are. You can find out what other resources they need. You can test new ideas and get feedback before you invest time in creating something nobody wants.

This creates a feedback loop that makes everything else easier. Instead of guessing what your audience wants, you can ask them directly. Instead of creating content in a vacuum, you can create content that responds to real questions from real people.

I started doing this with my podcast, and within six months, my email list had grown from zero to over 500 people. But more importantly, these weren't random email addresses. These were people who had actively chosen to engage with my content beyond just consuming it.

When I sent emails to this list, the open rates were much higher than industry averages. When I asked questions, people actually responded. When I eventually created paid offers, people bought them.

The podcast was at the top of the funnel – it attracted people who were interested in my topic. But the email list was where the real relationship-building happened. That's where I could have ongoing conversations, provide deeper value, and eventually make offers that people actually wanted.

This is the difference between having an audience and having a community. An audience consumes your content. A community participates in your world.

Every piece of content you create should have a clear next step for people who want to go deeper. Every blog post should offer a related resource. Every video should point to a useful tool. Every podcast episode should provide a way for engaged listeners to continue the conversation.

Don't leave this to chance. Don't assume people will just remember to come back next week. Give them a reason to give you their contact information right now while they're most engaged with what you have to say.

This is how you turn casual content consumption into real business relationships. This is how you build an asset that you own instead of just creating content for other people's platforms.

## Email Nurturing in Practice

Once you start building that email list, you need to do something with it. And this is where most people make a huge mistake.

They think email marketing means sending out a weekly newsletter with random tips and hoping people stay subscribed. Or they think it means immediately pitching their services to everyone who joins their list.

Both of those approaches miss the point entirely.

The real power of email marketing lies in automation. It's in creating a system that nurtures new subscribers by taking them through a logical sequence of content that builds trust, demonstrates value, and naturally leads to your offers.

Here's how this works in practice: When someone subscribes to your list by downloading that podcast resource we talked about, they don't just get added to your general newsletter. They get enrolled in a specific email sequence that's designed to introduce them to your world in the most logical way possible.

This is where your podcast episodes become incredibly valuable in a new way. Instead of people discovering your content randomly based on when they find you, every new subscriber can start at the beginning and work their way through your best content in the order that makes the most sense.

Let me show you exactly how to set this up.

Let's say you have 50 podcast episodes, but episodes 5, 12, 18, 24, and 31 are your absolute best ones — the episodes that really showcase your expertise and provide the most value. These become the foundation of your email nurture sequence.

When someone joins your list, they get an immediate email with the resource they requested. But then, over the next couple of weeks, they get a series of emails that introduce them to your best content.

**Email 1 (immediately):** Welcome email with the promised resource

**Email 2 (3 days later):** "Here's the best place to start" — links to episode 5

**Email 3 (3 days later):** "The mistake everyone makes" — links to episode 12

**Email 4 (3 days later):** "The advanced strategy that changes everything" — links to episode 18

**Email 5 (1 week later):** "My most popular episode" — links to episode 24

**Email 6 (1 week later):** "The counterintuitive approach that works" — links to episode 31

Each email doesn't just link to the episode. It provides context. It explains why this particular episode is important. It sets up the key insight they're about to learn. It makes them excited to listen.

But here's the beautiful part: it doesn't matter when someone finds you or joins your list. Whether they discover you when you have 10 episodes or 100 episodes, they still get the same introduction to your world. They still start with your best content. They still get the same high-quality first impression.

This solves one of the biggest problems with podcasting: new listeners don't know where to start. If someone discovers your podcast and you have 80 episodes, they're probably not going to go back and listen to episode 1. They'll listen to the most recent episode, which might not be your best work, and they might not get hooked.

But when they go through your email sequence, you can guide them to exactly the content that will make the biggest impact. You can control their first impression. You can ensure they see your best work first.

This also means your podcast episodes are working for you 24/7, even the old ones. That great episode you recorded six months ago isn't just sitting there hoping someone discovers it. It's actively being promoted to new subscribers who are most likely to find it valuable.

Over time, you can expand this sequence. Maybe you add more emails that link to different types of content. Maybe you include case studies or success stories. Maybe you can add surveys to learn more about what people need.

The key is that every person who joins your list gets a consistent, high-quality introduction to your world. They get your best content served up in a logical order. They get multiple touchpoints that build familiarity and trust. And they get all of this without you having to do any additional work once the sequence is set up.

This is the power of scalable nurturing. Whether one person joins your list today or 100 people join your list today, they all get the same level of attention and value. Your best content is working to build relationships even while you sleep.

And here's what happens over time: people start binge-listening to your content because your emails are introducing them to episodes they never would have found otherwise. They go deeper into your world because you're making it easy for them to do so. They start to see you as someone who understands their problems and has solutions that work.

When you eventually make an offer to these people, it's not coming out of nowhere. It's the natural next step in a relationship you've been building systematically through valuable content delivered at the right time in the right order.

This is how you turn a podcast into a business asset instead of just a content marketing experiment.

### Creating with the Audience, Not Just For Them

Most content creators make a fundamental mistake: they create content in isolation, publish it, and hope people like it. They might get some engagement, but they're essentially guessing what their audience wants.

But what if you could eliminate the guesswork? What if you could create content that you knew your audience wanted before you even made it?

This is where the real magic happens. This is where you stop creating content for your audience and start creating content with your audience.

The difference is huge. When you create content for your audience, you're making assumptions about what they need. When you create content with your audience, you're responding to what they tell you they need.

Here's how to make this shift: Start asking questions and actually listening to the answers.

In your podcast episodes, don't just share information. Ask your listeners what they want to know. Say things like, "I'm planning the topics for next month's episodes. What's the biggest challenge you're facing right now that I could help you solve? Send me an email and let me know."

In your email newsletters, include surveys or simple questions. "What's one thing you wish you knew more about in this area?" or "What's the biggest obstacle preventing you from getting results?"

When people reply to your emails, respond back. Have actual conversations. Most content creators never respond to emails from their subscribers, so when you do, it creates an immediate connection.

Here's what started happening when I made this shift: People began telling me exactly what they wanted me to create. Instead of guessing what topics would be valuable, I had a list of requests from real people with real problems.

Someone would email me and say, "I loved your episode about time management, but I'm struggling with prioritizing when everything feels urgent. Could you do an episode about that?"

That's not just a content idea. That's a content idea that you know at least one person wants, and probably many more people want it but haven't asked for it yet.

So I'd create that episode, and I'd start it by saying, "This episode was requested by Sarah, who emailed me about struggling with prioritization when everything feels urgent. If this is something you struggle with too, this episode is for you."

Do you see what that does? It shows other listeners that I actually read my emails and respond to requests. It makes them more likely to send their own requests. It creates content that directly addresses real problems my audience is facing.

But it gets even better. Sometimes, people will ask questions that reveal opportunities for paid products or services. Someone might email and say, "I love your content about marketing, but I'm really struggling with the implementation. Do you offer any kind of coaching or done-for-you services?"

That's market research you couldn't buy. That person just told you there's demand for a service you haven't created yet. And they did it voluntarily because they trusted you enough to share their real problems. I started keeping a simple spreadsheet of every question, request, and comment I got from my audience. Patterns emerged quickly. The same types of questions kept coming up. The same challenges kept being mentioned.

Those patterns became the foundation for everything I created next. New podcast episodes, new lead magnets, new courses, new services. Everything was based on what my audience had actually told me they wanted.

This approach also creates incredible loyalty. When you create content that directly responds to someone's request, they feel heard. They feel like you care about their specific situation. They become advocates for your work because you've demonstrated that you actually listen.

And here's a bonus: when you ask your audience what they want, some of them will offer to help create it.

I've had listeners volunteer to be interviewed for episodes. I've had people offer to share their case studies. I've had subscribers introduce me to other experts who became guests on my show.

Your audience becomes your collaborators, not just your consumers.

This also helps with imposter syndrome and self-doubt. Instead of wondering if anyone cares about what you have to say, you're creating content that people have specifically requested. You know there's demand because someone took the time to ask for it. The key is to make this two-way communication easy and natural. Always give people a way to respond. Always follow up when they do respond. Always look for patterns in what they're telling you.

Your audience will tell you exactly what to create next if you just ask them and listen to their answers.

## Refined Offers and Pricing Strategy

Once you've built this foundation of audience engagement and feedback, you're in a position that most business owners never reach: you actually know what people want to buy.

Most entrepreneurs create products and services based on what they think people need or what they think they'd be good at delivering. Then, they struggle to find customers for what they've created.

But when you've been having ongoing conversations with your audience, collecting their questions and requests, and understanding their real problems and frustrations, you can create offers that people actually want.

This is where all that audience research pays off. You're not guessing what to offer or how to price it. You're responding to market demand, which you can see and measure.

Let me share a framework that will help you think about this correctly. First, understand that people don't buy products or services. They buy outcomes. They buy the result they want to achieve or the problem they want to solve. Your job is to figure out what outcome your audience wants most and then create the most efficient path to deliver that outcome.

Here's how to find that out: Look at the patterns in the questions and requests you've been collecting. What underlying outcome are people really asking for?

Maybe they're asking about time management, productivity systems, and work-life balance. The outcome they really want is to feel in control of their schedule and reduce stress.

Maybe they're asking about marketing strategies, social media tactics, and lead generation. The outcome they really want is to get more customers consistently.

Maybe they're asking about meal planning, exercise routines, and healthy habits. The outcome they really want is to feel confident in their body and have more energy.

Once you identify the core outcome people want, you can create different ways to deliver that outcome at different price points and commitment levels.

**Low-ticket offer:** A resource that helps them make immediate progress. Maybe it's a checklist, a template, a short course, or a simple tool. Something they can buy for $10-50 and get value from right away.

**Mid-ticket offer:** A more comprehensive solution that requires more time and effort from them. Maybe it's a full course, a group program, or a mastermind. Something in the $200-2000 range that delivers deeper results.

**High-ticket offer:** A done-with-you or done-for-you solution where you're personally involved in helping them achieve the outcome. Maybe it's consulting, coaching, or custom services. Something in the $2000+ range where they get your direct attention and expertise.

The key is that all three levels solve the same core problem and deliver the same basic outcome. The difference is the level of support, the speed of results, and the amount of effort required from the customer.

Now, let's talk about pricing. This is where most people get it wrong.

They either price too low because they don't think anyone will pay more, or they price randomly based on what their competitors are charging, or they calculate their costs and add a markup.

None of those approaches work.

Here's the truth about pricing: people value what they pay for. If you price something too low, people will assume it's not very valuable. If you price it appropriately for the value you're delivering, people will take it seriously and get better results.

Your goal isn't to be the cheapest option. Your goal is to deliver so much value that your price feels like a bargain.

Here's a simple test for whether your pricing is right: Can your customers defend your price to other people involved in the decision?

If someone buys your course for $500, can they explain to their spouse why it was worth $500? If someone hires you for consulting at $200/hour, can they explain to their boss why that was a good investment?

If they can't defend your price, it means you haven't communicated the value clearly, or you haven't delivered enough value, or your price really is too high.

But if they can easily explain why it was worth every penny, you know you've got it right.

This is also why the feedback loop we talked about earlier is so important. When you're constantly getting input from your audience, you can test different price points and see how people respond.

You can ask directly: "I'm thinking about creating a course that walks through this entire process step-by-step. What would you expect to pay for something like that?"

You'll get a range of answers, but you'll also get a sense of what people think is reasonable. More importantly, you'll get a sense of how they think about the value of what you're offering.

Remember: your audience has already told you what problems they're struggling with and what outcomes they want to achieve. Now, you just need to create the most efficient path to deliver those outcomes and price it based on the value of the result, not the effort it takes you to deliver it.

If your course saves someone 40 hours of trial and error, it's worth more than if it saves them 4 hours. If your consulting helps someone make an extra $50,000 this year, it's worth more than if it helps them save $5,000.

Price is based on value delivered, not time invested.

## From Prospects to Paying Clients

At this point, you've built something remarkable: a system that consistently attracts the right people, nurtures them with valuable content, builds real relationships through two-way communication, and creates offers based on what they've actually told you they want.

Now, it's time to connect all these pieces into a conversion system that naturally turns prospects into paying clients.

The beautiful thing about doing all this foundational work is that selling becomes much easier. You're not trying to convince strangers to buy something they're not sure they need. You're offering solutions to people who have already demonstrated interest in what you provide.

Here's how the pieces fit together:

Someone discovers your content (podcast, blog, video, speaking, etc.) and finds value in it. They download a resource from you in exchange for their email address. They go through your nurture sequence and consume your best content. They start to see you as someone who understands their problems and has solutions that work.

Then, they engage with you directly. Maybe they reply to one of your emails. Maybe they leave a comment on your podcast. Maybe they reach out with a question. This is where the relationship shifts from one-way to two-way.

As you continue to provide value and stay in regular contact, they start to think of you when their problem becomes urgent enough that they need to solve it now, not someday.

And that's when they're ready to buy.

But here's where most people make a mistake: they assume people will just reach out and ask to hire them when they're ready. But most people don't do that. They need a clear pathway to take the next step.

This is where you need to be intentional about creating conversion opportunities.

The simplest way to do this is through consultations or strategy calls. In your emails and content, you periodically mention that you offer free strategy calls where you help people create a custom plan for achieving their goals.

This isn't a sales call where you pitch your services. It's a genuine consulting call where you provide value and help them think through their situation. But if it becomes clear that you can help them implement the strategy you've outlined, that's when you can mention your paid services.

The key is that by the time someone books a call with you, they already know, like, and trust you. They've been consuming your content. They've been on your email list. They've seen that you know what you're talking about. The call isn't about convincing them that you're competent. It's about determining whether you can help them solve their specific problem.

Another approach is to create low-ticket offers that serve as natural stepping stones to higher-ticket services. That $50 template pack or $200 course isn't just a product – it's also a way for people to experience working with you before making a bigger commitment.

When someone buys your low-ticket offer and gets great results, they become a warm prospect for your higher-ticket services. They've already experienced the quality of your work. They trust that you can deliver what you promise.

This is also where testimonials and case studies become incredibly powerful. Every successful client gives you proof that your approach works. Every great result becomes evidence that you can deliver similar results for similar people.

But here's the key: don't just collect testimonials that say you're great to work with. Collect testimonials that focus on the specific results people achieved. Numbers, timelines, and concrete outcomes are much more powerful than general praise.

"Working with Sarah was amazing; she's so knowledgeable and helpful." This is nice, but it doesn't tell prospects what they can expect.

"Sarah helped me increase my monthly revenue from $3,000 to $8,000 in four months by implementing the client attraction system she taught me" is much more compelling because it shows a specific result that other people can relate to.

The nurturing system you've built naturally feeds prospects into your conversion process. The relationships you've developed through two-way communication make the selling conversation easier. The offers you've created based on audience feedback are more likely to be what people actually want to buy.

Most importantly, you're not selling to strangers. You're offering solutions to people who already know you, trust you, and have a relationship with you.

This is how selling should feel: natural, helpful, and focused on solving real problems for real people.

## The Power of Ecosystems and Partnerships

Here's something that can transform your business faster than almost anything else: understanding that your clients need more than just what you offer.

Think about it: your clients have problems before they find you, and they have different problems after they work with you. They need solutions you don't provide, and they need ongoing support after you've solved their initial problem.

Most business owners see this as a limitation. They think they need to expand their services to meet every need their clients have. But that's a mistake. You can't be everything to everyone, and trying to do so will dilute your expertise and confuse your message.

Instead, you should think of the ecosystem. Who else serves your ideal client before they need you? Who serves them after they work with you? Who serves them at the same time they're working with you but in a different capacity?

These are your potential strategic partners.

Let me give you some examples:

If you're a business coach who helps people start their first business, your clients probably need an accountant, a lawyer, a web designer, a copywriter, and maybe a business bank account. These are all services you don't provide, but your clients definitely need them.

If you're a fitness trainer, your clients might also need a nutritionist, a massage therapist, a meal prep service, and maybe supplements or workout gear.

If you're a marketing consultant, your clients might need a graphic designer, a web developer, a photographer, a videographer, and various software tools.

Instead of seeing these as competitors or irrelevant services, see them as partnership opportunities.

Here's how this works: You build relationships with high-quality providers in these adjacent areas. You get to know their work, understand their approach, and confirm that they deliver great results for their clients.

Then, when your clients need these services, you refer them to your partners. And when your partners' clients need what you offer, they refer them to you.

This creates a referral ecosystem where everyone wins. Your clients get connected with trusted providers for the services they need. Your partners get qualified referrals from someone they trust. And you get referrals from multiple sources instead of having to generate all your leads yourself.

But here's the key: this has to be genuine. You can't just partner with anyone who's willing to refer people to you. You need to partner with people who share your standards and values, who deliver excellent work, and who treat their clients the way you treat yours.

Your reputation is tied to the people you recommend. If you refer someone to a web designer who does sloppy work or treats clients poorly, that reflects on you. But if you refer someone to a web designer who does amazing work and makes your client's life easier, you look like a hero.

Start by making a list of all the services your ideal client needs throughout their journey. Think about what they need before they find you, what they need while they're working with you, and what they need after they achieve their initial goal with you.

Then, start researching who provides those services in your area or online. Look for people who serve the same type of client you serve but at a different stage of their journey or with a different type of solution.

Reach out and introduce yourself. Explain what you do, who you serve, and that you're looking to build relationships with other service providers who serve similar clients. Most people are open to this because they understand the value of having trusted referral sources.

Start small. Maybe you have coffee with a few potential partners and get to know their approach. Maybe you refer one client to them and see how it goes. Maybe you can collaborate on a piece of content or a joint workshop.

Over time, these relationships can become one of your most valuable business assets. I know business owners who get 50% or more of their new clients from referral partners. They spend less time on marketing and lead generation because their network consistently sends them qualified prospects.

But this only works if you're equally committed to sending referrals to your partners. It's not about finding people who will refer business to you. It's about building genuine relationships where everyone is looking out for each other's success.

This also positions you as more than just another service provider. You become a trusted advisor who can connect your clients with solutions for all their needs. You become the center of their professional network instead of just one vendor they work with.

Think about the difference in how clients perceive these two scenarios:

Scenario 1: They work with you for your specific service, and when they need other services, they're on their own to find providers and hope they're good.

Scenario 2: They work with you for your specific service, and when they need other services, you connect them with trusted partners who you know will take great care of them.

In which scenario are you more valuable? In which scenario are they more likely to refer other people to you?

The ecosystem approach makes you more valuable to your clients and creates multiple streams of referrals for your business. It's one of the most effective ways to grow without having to constantly chase new leads.

## Retention: Serve Deeply, Not Just Broadly

Most business owners are obsessed with getting new customers. They spend all their time and energy on marketing, lead generation, and conversion. But they're missing the biggest opportunity in their business: the customers they already have.

Here's a simple truth that can transform your business: it's much easier and more profitable to serve existing customers more deeply than it is to constantly find new customers.

Yet most service providers treat their clients like one-time transactions. They solve the immediate problem, collect their fee, and then start looking for the next client. This is exhausting, unpredictable, and leaves massive amounts of money on the table.

What if instead of constantly chasing new customers, you focused on becoming indispensable to the customers you already have?

This is the difference between market share and wallet share. Market share is about getting a piece of everyone's business. Wallet sharing is about getting more of each customer's business.

Most businesses compete for market share. They try to get more customers, more visibility, and more leads. However, the businesses that really thrive focus on wallet share. They become so valuable to their existing customers that those customers give them more and more of their business over time.

Here's what this looks like in practice:

Instead of just solving one problem for a client and moving on, you become their go-to resource for everything related to your area of expertise. Instead of being a vendor, they hire occasionally. You become a trusted advisor to whom they turn regularly. Let's say you're a marketing consultant who helps small businesses with their social media strategy. The typical approach would be to work with a client for a few months, help them set up their social media systems, and then move on to the next client.

However, the wallet share approach would be different. After you help them with social media, you notice they're struggling with email marketing. So you offer to help with that too. Then you notice their website needs work. Then their sales process could be improved. Then, they need help training their team.

Each of these becomes an opportunity to serve them more deeply instead of just serving more people superficially.

This approach has several huge advantages:

First, it's more predictable. Instead of constantly worrying about where your next client will come from, you have ongoing relationships that generate ongoing revenue.

Second, it's more profitable. You've already built trust and rapport with these clients. You understand their business and their challenges. The sales process for additional services is much shorter and easier than finding and converting new clients.

Third, it creates better results for your clients. Instead of getting help from multiple disconnected service providers, they get integrated solutions from someone who understands their entire situation.

Fourth, it makes your clients more successful, which leads to better testimonials, more referrals, and a stronger reputation in your market.

But here's the key: this only works if you deliver exceptional results consistently. You can't just keep selling more services to the same people. You have to prove your value over and over again.

This is where the concept of a "world-class experience" becomes crucial. Every interaction your clients have with you should be predictable, repeatable, and consistently excellent.

They should know what to expect when they work with you. They should get regular updates on progress. They should feel like their investment is paying off. They should see measurable results that justify continuing to work with you.

Most service providers are inconsistent. Sometimes, they're responsive and thorough. Sometimes, they're slow and sloppy. Sometimes they over-deliver. Sometimes they under-deliver. This inconsistency makes clients nervous about investing more money with them.

But when you create systems that ensure every client gets the same high-quality experience, they start to trust that working with you will always be a good investment.

This means documenting your processes, setting clear expectations, following through on commitments, and proactively communicating throughout every project.

It means treating each client like they're your only client, even when you're serving multiple people.

It means going slightly above and beyond what you promised consistently rather than occasionally going way above and beyond and, at other times, falling short.

When you master this, something interesting happens: clients start asking you what else you can help them with. Instead of you having to sell additional services, they start requesting them.

"We're so happy with how the marketing project turned out. Do you also help with sales training?"

"This social media strategy is working great. Can you help us improve our email newsletters, too?"

"You understand our business so well. What do you think we should focus on next?"

This is the goal: becoming so valuable to your existing clients that they can't imagine working with anyone else for anything related to what you do.

## Creating a Referral Engine

Let's talk about something that most business owners completely mess up: asking for referrals.

Most people either never ask for referrals at all, or they ask in a way that's awkward and ineffective. They'll finish a project with a client and say something like, "If you know anyone else who could use my services, please send them my way."

That's not a referral request. That's a hope and a prayer.

Here's the problem: even your happiest clients won't refer people to you unless you make it easy and give them a specific reason to do it.

But before we talk about how to ask for referrals, let's talk about why people make referrals in the first place.

People don't make referrals to help you grow your business. They make referrals to help their friends and colleagues solve problems. They make referrals to look good and be helpful to people they care about.

This is a crucial distinction. When you understand that referrals are about your clients wanting to help other people, not about them wanting to help you, everything changes. There's also a psychological concept, I've already mentioned, called Dunbar's Number that's incredibly useful here. Research suggests that people can only maintain meaningful relationships with about 150 people, but they have looser social connections with about 275 people in total. That means every one of your clients is connected to roughly 275 other people. Some of those people probably have the same problems your client had before they found you.

Your job is to help your clients identify those people and give them an easy way to connect them with you.

Here's how to do this effectively:

First, help your clients recognize when someone in their network might need your help. Most people don't naturally think about referring business unless you train them to notice the opportunities.

Give your clients specific phrases to listen for. Things like:

"I hate dealing with..."

"I'm so frustrated with..."

"I wish I could find someone who..."

"Do you know anyone who can help with..."

When they hear these phrases related to problems you solve, that's a referral opportunity.

Second, make it easy for them to make the referral. Don't expect them to remember your website or explain what you do. Give them tools that make the referral process simple.

This could be a simple one-page overview of what you do and how to contact you. It could be a short video they can share that explains your services. It could be a specific landing page they can direct people to.

Third, give them social currency. Make them look good when making the referral.

This means being exceptional at what you do, obviously. However, it also means following up with both your client and the referred prospect to let them know what happened.

If someone refers a prospect to you, reach out to both people. Thank your client for the referral. Let them know you connected with their friend and what the next steps are. Make them feel good about making the introduction.

Even if the referred prospect doesn't become a client, follow up with your original client to let them know you appreciated the referral and how the conversation went.

This creates a positive feedback loop. When clients see that you handle their referrals professionally and keep them informed, they're more likely to make additional referrals in the future.

Fourth, ask at the right time. The best time to ask for referrals is right after you've delivered a great result. When your clients are excited about what you've accomplished together, that's when they're most likely to think of other people who could benefit from your help.

Don't wait until the project is completely over and they've moved on to other things. Ask when the success is fresh and when they're feeling grateful for your help.

Here's a simple script that works:

"I'm so glad we were able to [specific result you achieved]. I know this is going to make a big difference for your business. I'm curious - do you know other [type of business] owners who are struggling with [the problem you solved]? I'd love to help them get similar results."

Notice that this isn't about asking them to promote your business. It's about asking them to help other people who have the same problem they used to have.

Fifth, create systematic touchpoints where referrals naturally come up. Don't just ask for referrals once and then never bring it up again.

In your regular check-ins with clients, you can casually mention success stories from other clients (without violating confidentiality) and ask if they know anyone dealing with similar challenges.

In your newsletters or email updates, you can share case studies and mention that you're currently accepting new clients who fit a specific profile.

The key is making referrals a natural part of your ongoing relationship with clients, not an awkward one-time ask.

When you do this consistently and systematically, referrals become a predictable part of your business growth instead of a random lucky break that occasionally happens.

I know business owners who get 3-5 qualified referrals every month just by implementing these simple systems. They don't have to spend as much time and money on marketing because their clients are consistently sending them ideal prospects.

But it only works if you're delivering exceptional results and making the referral process easy and natural for your clients.

## Common Mistakes to Avoid

After working with thousands of entrepreneurs over the years, I've seen the same mistakes over and over again. Most people sabotage their own success in predictable ways, and the frustrating thing is that these mistakes are completely avoidable if you know what to look for.

Let me walk you through the four most common ways people mess this up so you can avoid them.

**Mistake #1: Doing too much of the wrong things**

This is the "busy but broke" syndrome. People who make this mistake are constantly active. They're posting on social media every day. They're networking constantly. They're trying every new marketing tactic they hear about. They're working 60-hour weeks.

But they're not making money.

Why? Because they're confusing activity with progress. They're doing lots of stuff, but none of it is the right stuff.

They're posting content that doesn't connect with their ideal clients. They're networking with people who can't afford their services or don't need what they offer. They're implementing marketing tactics that might work for other businesses but don't make sense for their situation.

This usually happens because they're trying to copy what they see other successful people doing without understanding why those tactics work for those specific people in those specific situations.

Or they're following generic business advice that sounds logical but isn't tailored to their unique circumstances.

The fix: Focus on the fundamentals we've covered in this book. Get crystal clear on your market, your message, and your medium. Build systems that work for your specific situation instead of trying to do everything.

## Mistake #2: Not doing anything due to fear or perfectionism

This is the opposite problem, but it's just as destructive. These are the people who consume endless amounts of business content but never actually implement any of it.

They read every book, take every course, listen to every podcast, but they never start their own podcast, never send their first newsletter, and never make their first offer.

They're waiting until they know enough, or until they have the perfect plan, or until they feel confident, or until the timing is right.

But here's the truth: you'll never feel ready. You'll never have perfect information. There will never be a perfect time to start.

The people who succeed are the ones who start before they feel ready and figure it out as they go.

This mistake usually stems from fear of failure, fear of judgment, or fear of success. People are so worried about doing it wrong that they never do anything at all.

The fix: Start before you're ready. Embrace the fact that your first attempts will be imperfect. Focus on progress, not perfection. Remember that you can't steer a parked car – you have to be moving to make course corrections.

## Mistake #3: Thinking about doing it but never starting

This is a variation of mistake #2 but with a different flavor. These people have great intentions and detailed plans. They think about their business constantly. They make lists, set goals, and buy planners.

But they never actually do the work.

They'll spend hours researching podcast equipment but never record an episode. They'll plan out an entire content calendar but never publish a single piece of content. They'll design elaborate marketing funnels but never drive any traffic to them.

This happens because thinking about doing something gives you some of the psychological satisfaction of actually doing it without any of the risk or effort.

Planning feels productive. It feels like progress. But planning without execution is just procrastination in disguise.

The fix: Set implementation deadlines that are uncomfortably soon. Force yourself to publish something imperfect rather than planning something perfect that never sees the light of day. Focus on taking action, even small actions, every single day.

## Mistake #4: Not thinking at all – just winging it

On the other end of the spectrum, you have people who take massive action but without any strategy or plan.

They start podcasting without defining their target audience. They create offers without understanding what their market actually wants. They launch websites without thinking about how people will find them.

This approach usually leads to a lot of wasted effort and frustration. They work hard but don't see results because they're shooting in the dark.

The fix: Find the balance between planning and action. Do enough thinking and research to make sure you're pointed in the right direction, but don't get stuck in analysis paralysis. Plan, then act, then adjust based on what you learn.

Here's the thing: all four of these mistakes come from the same root cause – not having a clear, systematic approach to building your business.

When you don't have a proven framework to follow, you either do too much random stuff, you get paralyzed by all the options, you overthink everything, or you just wing it and hope for the best.

But when you have a clear system – like the one we've outlined in this book – you know exactly what to focus on and what to ignore. You know what the next step is. You have a roadmap that guides your decisions and actions.

The solution to all of these mistakes is the same: follow a proven system, take consistent action, and adjust based on your results.

If you're not sure which mistake you're making, or if you want a more specific diagnosis of what's holding you back, take the Online Prosperity Quiz. It's a free assessment that will identify your specific obstacles and give you a customized action plan for overcoming them.

You can find it at www.mediamogulsclub.com.au or scan the QR code at the end of this chapter.

The quiz takes about 5 minutes and will save you months of trial and error by showing you exactly where to focus your efforts.

# Conclusion

We've covered a lot of ground together. When you started reading this book, you might have felt overwhelmed by all the different pieces involved in building an online business. The market research, message development, the content creation, lead generation, nurturing, and sales processes can feel like a lot.

But look how far you've come.

You now understand how to identify and connect with your ideal market instead of trying to appeal to everyone. You know how to craft a message that actually resonates with real people who have real problems you can solve. You've learned how to choose and master a medium that plays to your strengths and reaches your audience where they already are.

You understand how to generate leads consistently instead of hoping people will magically find you. You know how to nurture those leads into genuine relationships built on trust and value. You've learned how to create offers based on what your audience actually wants, not just what you think they need.

You understand the power of building your own platform instead of relying on rented attention from social media. You know how to turn passive consumers into active community members. You've learned how to create systems that work for you 24/7, even while you sleep.

Most importantly, you've learned that building a successful online business isn't about having some special talent or secret knowledge that most people don't have. It's about following a proven system, taking consistent action, and adjusting based on your results.

You have everything you need to succeed. The only question is: what are you going to do with it?

Here's what I want you to understand: you are closer than you think you are to creating the business and lifestyle you want.

Most people who feel stuck or overwhelmed aren't actually that far from a breakthrough. They're usually just one or two systematic changes away from everything clicking into place.

Maybe you need to finally start that podcast you've been thinking about for months. Maybe you need to create your first lead magnet and start building your email list. Maybe you need to reach out to potential partners and start building referral relationships.

Maybe you just need to stop consuming business content and start implementing what you already know.

The biggest tragedy in business isn't people who try and fail. It's people who never try at all because they're waiting for the perfect moment or the perfect plan or the perfect confidence level that never comes.

Don't be one of those people.

Your audience is out there right now, looking for someone who understands their problems and has solutions that work. They're searching for content, asking questions in Facebook groups, listening to podcasts, reading blogs, and trying to figure out how to solve the challenges you could help them with.

But they can't find you if you don't put yourself out there.

They can't hire you if you don't make offers.

They can't refer people to you if you don't ask.

They can't become raving fans if you don't give them something to rave about.

The world doesn't need another person who knows how to build a business. The world needs you to actually build yours.

Stop overthinking. Stop underacting. Stop waiting for permission, perfect conditions, or complete confidence.

Start doing what matters most.

Create content that helps people. Build relationships with your audience. Make offers that solve real problems.

Follow up consistently. Ask for referrals. Partner with other businesses. Serve your clients deeply.

Do the work, and the results will follow.

But here's the most important thing: *remember why you started this journey in the first place.*

It probably wasn't just about making money, although financial freedom is certainly important. It was probably about having the freedom to work on your own terms, to serve people in a way that feels meaningful, to build something that matters.

It was about creating a business that supports the lifestyle you want instead of consuming your entire life.

It was about using your knowledge and experience to make a difference in other people's lives.

That vision is still possible. In fact, it's more possible now than when you started because now you have a roadmap for getting there.

The business you want to build is not an impossible dream. It's the logical result of implementing the systems and strategies we've covered in this book.

Other people with less experience, fewer resources, and more obstacles have built successful online businesses using these exact principles. There's no reason you can't do the same.

The only thing standing between where you are now and where you want to be is implementation.

So stop reading about building a business and start actually building one.

Your future clients are waiting for you.

Your ideal lifestyle is waiting for you.

The impact you want to make is waiting for you.

But none of it will happen until you stop waiting and start doing.

The time is now. The opportunity is here. The path is clear.

All that's left is for you to take the first step.

And then the next one.

And then the next one.

One day, you look back and realize you've built exactly the business and life you dreamed about when you first started this journey.

That day can come sooner than you think.

But only if you start today.

So what are you waiting for?

**#ownyourmedia**

www.ingramcontent.com/pod-product-compliance
Lightning Source LLC
Chambersburg PA
CBHW061157240326
R18026500001B/R180265PG41519CBX00023B/39